King Lear

ARDEN STUDENT SKILLS: LANGUAGE AND WRITING

Series Editor
Dympna Callaghan, Syracuse University

Published Titles
A Midsummer Night's Dream, R. S. White
As You Like It, Abigail Rokison-Woodall
Antony and Cleopatra, Virginia Mason Vaughan
Hamlet, Dympna Callaghan
King Richard III, Rebecca Lemon
Macbeth, Emma Smith
Much Ado about Nothing, Indira Ghose
Othello, Laurie Maguire
Romeo and Juliet, Catherine Belsey
The Tempest, Brinda Charry
Twelfth Night, Frances E. Dolan

Forthcoming Titles
The Winter's Tale, Mario DiGangi

King Lear

Language and Writing

JEAN E. HOWARD

THE ARDEN SHAKESPEARE
LONDON • NEW YORK • OXFORD • NEW DELHI • SYDNEY

THE ARDEN SHAKESPEARE
Bloomsbury Publishing Plc
50 Bedford Square, London, WC1B 3DP, UK
1385 Broadway, New York, NY 10018, USA
29 Earlsfort Terrace, Dublin 2, Ireland

BLOOMSBURY, THE ARDEN SHAKESPEARE and the Arden Shakespeare
logo are trademarks of Bloomsbury Publishing Plc

First published in Great Britain 2022

Cover design: Tjaša Krivec
Cover image © The British Library Board (1.4.217-21)

A catalogue record for this book is available from the British Library.

A catalog record for this book is available from the Library of Congress.

ISBN: HB: 978-1-4725-1836-1
PB: 978-1-4081-8227-7
ePDF: 978-1-4081-8228-4
eBook: 978-1-4081-8229-1

Series: Arden Student Skills: Language and Writing

Typeset by RefineCatch Limited, Bungay, Suffolk
Printed and bound in Great Britain

To find out more about our authors and books visit www.bloomsbury.com
and sign up for our newsletters.

For Eleanor, Caroline and Margaret, the Best of Girls

CONTENTS

SERIES EDITOR'S PREFACE

This series puts the pedagogical expertise of distinguished literary critics at the disposal of students embarking upon Shakespeare Studies at university. While they demonstrate a variety of approaches to the plays, all the contributors to the series share a deep commitment to teaching and a wealth of knowledge about the culture and history of Shakespeare's England. The approach of each of the volumes is direct yet intellectually sophisticated and tackles the challenges Shakespeare presents. These volumes do not provide a shortcut to Shakespeare's works but instead offer a careful explication of them directed towards students' own processing and interpretation of the plays and poems.

Students' needs in relation to Shakespeare revolve overwhelmingly around language, and Shakespeare's language is what most distinguishes him from his rivals and collaborators – as well as what most embeds him in his own historical moment. The Language and Writing series understands language as the very heart of Shakespeare's literary achievement rather than as an obstacle to be circumvented. This series addresses the difficulties often encountered in reading Shakespeare alongside the necessity of writing papers for university examinations and course assessment. The primary objective here is to foster rigorous critical engagement with the texts by helping students develop their own critical writing skills. Language and Writing titles demonstrate how to develop students' own capacity to articulate and enlarge upon their experience of encountering the text, far beyond summarizing, paraphrasing or 'translating' Shakespeare's language into a more palatable, contemporary form. Each of the volumes in the series introduces the text as an act of specifically literary language and shows that the multifarious issues of life and history that Shakespeare's work addresses cannot be separated from their expression in language. In addition, each book takes students through a series of guidelines about how to develop viable undergraduate critical essays on the text in question, not by delivering interpretations but rather by taking readers step by step through the process of discovering and developing their own critical ideas.

All the books include chapters examining the text from the point of view of its composition, that is, from the perspective of Shakespeare's own process of composition as a reader, thinker and writer. The opening chapters consider when and how the play was written, addressing, for example, the extant literary and cultural acts of language, from which Shakespeare constructed his work – including his sources – as well as the generic, literary and theatrical conventions at his disposal. Subsequent sections demonstrate how to engage in detailed examination and analysis of the text and focus on the literary, technical and historical intricacies of Shakespeare's verse and prose. Each volume also includes some discussion of performance. Other chapters cover textual issues as well as the interpretation of the extant texts for any given play on stage and screen, treating, for example, the use of stage directions or parts of the play that are typically cut in performance. Authors also address issues of stage/ film history as they relate to the cultural evolution of Shakespeare's words. In addition, these chapters deal with the critical reception of the work, particularly the newer theoretical and historicist approaches that have revolutionized our understanding of Shakespeare's language over the past forty years. Crucially, every chapter contains a section on 'Writing matters', which links the analysis of Shakespeare's language with students' own critical writing.

The series empowers students to read and write about Shakespeare with scholarly confidence and hopes to inspire their enthusiasm for doing so. The authors in this series have been selected because they combine scholarly distinction with outstanding teaching skills. Each book exposes the reader to an eminent scholar's teaching in action and expresses a vocational commitment to making Shakespeare accessible to a new generation of student readers.

Professor Dympna Callaghan
Series Editor
Arden Student Skills: Language and Writing

PREFACE

King Lear is the most elemental of Shakespeare's tragedies. By this I mean not only that it exposes its characters to earth, air, wind and fire, the four substances of which the cosmos, and all bodies, were believed to be composed, but also that it elicits in those characters elemental emotions of terror, fury, love and despair. For audiences, the experience of reading or viewing *King Lear* has over centuries been recognized as uniquely harrowing.

To a degree unusual in Shakespeare's plays, many characters in *King Lear* live 'unhoused' for long periods of time. As such, they endure wind, rain, heat, cold and hunger. Poor Tom, Lear, Kent, the Fool – for much of the play they lack shelter, decent food and all the affordances of what we assume civilized life to be. Many people in this play live close to beasts, forcing the question of what distinguishes humanity from the other creatures with whom it shares the earth. It also forces the question of why the benefits of a sheltered life should be so unevenly distributed. Why should some people live in castles and wear furred gowns while others, clothed in rags, struggle unprotected against the physical elements? Questions of justice and the proper distribution of worldly resources permeate the play. Why do some have so much, and some so little? Who is responsible for creating a more just social order? Is it the gods, or is it humans themselves?

In *Lear* Shakespeare does not shrink from depicting humanity's capacity for inhumanity. Selfishness, cruelty, thoughtless entitlement and the will to power are all on display. So, however, are acts of kindness and care, often performed by those who have everything to lose by defying their social betters and nothing to gain but the satisfaction of acting in accord with their own ethical beliefs. The play thus forces another question: why do high rank, political power and wealth not align with goodness and morality? Is it possible to make them align more closely?

In this book I hope you will find tools and strategies for exploring the political and ethical questions that lie at the heart of this tragedy. Our focus will be on the play's language, language meaning both the words spoken by the play's characters and also the performance elements that Shakespeare uses to convey meaning. Costume, gesture and physical props are all part of the language of performance, a language you will learn how to read as deftly as you will engage with the rhetorical devices that give shape to a soliloquy or a dialogue among several characters. You will also learn to read the language of a play's structure, such as the potential meanings released by juxtaposing one scene against another or by repeating and revising patterns of physical interaction across a whole play. Drama is an exciting medium because it communicates and embodies potential meanings in multiple ways. When we read a play we probably first pay attention to its verbal texture, but a playscript also points to performance. It helps us to imagine how the work might look and sound when actors don costumes and begin to embody their parts. I hope in what follows to expand your sense of what it means to read the languages in which *King Lear* speaks to us.

As you read this book, remember to trust yourself and your responses. This book focuses on techniques for reading a play as complex as *King Lear*, but these techniques are only a means to an end. The end is your own critical engagement with the text, the arguments you are spurred to make about it, and the pleasure you take in meeting its emotional and intellectual challenges. Let's begin.

Introduction

'Howl, howl, howl, howl!'[1] King Lear cries as he makes his final entry in the tragedy that bears his name. His words follow the stage direction that reads: '*Enter* LEAR *with* CORDELIA *in his arms*.' Cordelia is Lear's beloved daughter, and she has been killed by her enemies. Given that context, what can we say about Lear's words here? First, of course, a howl is a cry of anguish, but it is also a sound a wolf, as well as a human, might make. It suggests a person at the limits of human speech, howling like a beast. *Howl* can also be a command, an imperative. But whom might Lear be ordering to howl – himself, the courtiers who surround him on the stage, or perhaps the elements themselves? Winds also howl, and the middle scenes of this tragedy contain one of the most famous storms in all of literature. Does Lear's language here recall that storm and transpose it from a physical to a psychic condition? Does a storm of grief now replace a storm of wind and rain? And who can help Lear calm *this* storm?

This use of *howl*, its importance driven home by four urgent repetitions of the same word, suggests something of the elemental quality of one of Shakespeare's greatest tragedies. People in *King Lear* suffer unspeakably, and much of the suffering stems from the actions of intimates – children and servants and parents. People

---

[1] All references to *King Lear*, unless otherwise noted, will be to the third edition of the *Arden Shakespeare* third series edition of the play. Ed. R. A. Foakes (London: Bloomsbury, 1997), here cited at 5.3.255, p. 385.

suffer in their bodies – they are blinded, cast out of doors in the middle of a storm, poisoned, killed in battle, hunted through the night; and they suffer in their minds – they are humiliated and shamed, feel guilt, go mad and in their torment seek their own deaths. Critics have called *Lear* a play that resonates with times of catastrophe. In the twentieth and twenty-first centuries it has often been staged, despite the difficulties of performing its emotional and physical rigours, because it seems an apt play for a time that has known two world wars, the Holocaust, the development of the atomic bomb, the forced migration of millions of victims of war and violence, and now the devastation caused by global warming and impending climate catastrophe. How do humans survive when the contours of their known worlds shatter and crumble? Are there gods above who care for mankind, or is the universe cruelly indifferent to human suffering? In extremity, is man just another beast, or does something remain that justifies humanity's claim to privileged and exceptional status?

Writing matters

In this book you will be invited to explore many aspects of this challenging play with the intent that eventually you will be prepared to address the biggest questions that it raises. Our surest route into the heart of the play is through its language. In the chapters that follow you will be asked to read *King Lear*'s language carefully, starting with individual words, short speeches, and sections of dialogue, and eventually considering word clusters and images that draw together the whole play. You will not only learn strategies for reading the play's language with new tools at your disposal, but also for writing about it. Writing is one of the ways in which every reader makes discoveries about texts. We find out what we think about a speech or an image by writing about it. It's also often a spur to our own thoughts to learn what other critics have said about a play, and how smart directors and actors have produced it. The annotated bibliography at the back of this book will point you towards some key articles and books bearing on *King Lear*; and in the third chapter we will introduce two film versions of the play that have excited the imaginations of readers and theatregoers.

Because of the complexity of *King Lear*, the rest of this chapter will lay out some basic information about the kind of play *Lear* is, its plot, and about its dramatic construction, sources, language, characters, themes, and the texts from which modern versions are constructed. Then we will begin to focus in greater depth on particular aspects of the play and your engagement with it as readers and writers.

Genre

King Lear is one of Shakespeare's tragedies, probably written in 1606 after he had produced some of his other major tragic plays, including *Hamlet* and *Othello*. It's important to recognize the play's status as a tragedy because a play's genre partly determines what an audience would have expected when it went to see a play. We know from contemporary accounts that when an early modern theatre company was performing a tragedy, members of the company would typically hang black curtains from the back wall of the stage to cue the audience as to the kind of theatrical experience being offered. Most often, early modern tragedy focuses on a story in which a protagonist or leading character becomes embroiled in a situation in which they make a decision or take an action that leads to their death. Not just anyone could be a tragic protagonist; most in this patriarchal culture were men, though a few were women. Monarchs, princes, generals or other important public figures – these were typically the leading characters of early modern tragedy. The protagonist's story, however, involved the whole community because the downfall of such an eminent figure had ramifications for the body politic as well as for the person's household and lineage.

Early modern tragic action thus has both scope and grandeur. It affects an important person and their community in a way that shakes that community to its foundations. Moreover, unlike comedy, which deals with more ordinary actions and situations, early modern tragedy offered its characters no second chances. The tragic decision or action taken by the protagonist leads to a series of consequences from which there is no turning back. That is why there is a certain terribleness to tragedy. Since Aristotle, it has typically been taken to arouse pity and terror in audiences, struck as they are by the spectacle of a noble person destroyed by fate or by his or her own choices. Sometimes, revenge is a motif in early modern tragedy. An eminent person's friend or family member is unjustly killed, and then the protagonist has to search out the murderer and bring them to justice, often working outside the law because the murderer is often an important figure who can block a proper legal investigation of the crime. Not all tragedies of the period are revenge tragedies, of course, but almost all involve bloodshed, murder and the psychic undoing of the main character.

Often, early modern tragedy raises the question of whether the protagonist learns something from their mistakes and suffering. A moral or sentimental view of tragedy argues that from tragic suffering comes self-knowledge, and while the protagonist is destroyed, that person has acquired valuable knowledge from this experience. *King Lear* is an interesting case in this regard. Its protagonist is 80 years old when the play opens. Can such an old man learn new things? How has this ruler gotten to be 80 years old and still be as unaware of the basics of good kingship and good parenting as Lear shows himself to be in the first scene of the play? What, if anything, does Lear 'learn' in the course of his journey through the play's five acts? Does he die illuminated by insight or in a mist of confusion? These are some of the most basic questions this book will invite you to explore, partly by focusing on the changing language of the old king throughout the play.

Plot

The play's plot has in some ways the simplicity of a fairy tale. An old King has three daughters, and he loves the youngest, Cordelia, best. Eighty years old and eager to shake off the responsibilities of kingship, King Lear poses a love test: each daughter must say how much she loves her father in order to receive a third of his kingdom as a reward. The two oldest, Goneril and Regan, comply; Cordelia demurs, and an angry Lear refuses to give her a portion of his kingdom. She leaves Britain with her husband-to-be, the King of France. Lear also banishes his loyal retainer, Kent, who opposes his master's foolish banishment of Cordelia. The two oldest daughters, who are by turns to shelter Lear and a hundred of his knights, determine to control their father and strip him of his expensive retinue. Eventually the furious old King flees from their perceived unkindness onto the storm-swept heath with only a handful of attendants, including the disguised Kent and the court fool, to keep him company. Exposed to the elements and consumed by rage and a sense of impotence, Lear goes mad, rescued from this madness primarily by the kindness of Cordelia who returns with soldiers from France to find her father and restore his rights. She is reunited with Lear, but then is imprisoned and hung, at which point Lear himself dies of weariness and grief. The two older sisters also die, having fallen out over the sexual favours of Edmund, a central figure in the play's second plot.

In this second plot, the Earl of Gloucester, a figure loyal to Lear, is tricked by his illegitimate son Edmund into believing his legitimate son, Edgar, has betrayed him. Edgar escapes the men Gloucester sends to apprehend him by disguising himself as Poor Tom, a mad beggar. Wandering in a nearly naked state on the heath, he encounters Lear in the storm and for a while becomes part of the old King's party of lost souls. Meanwhile, Edmund tells Regan's husband, the Duke of Cornwall, that Gloucester is plotting to help Lear regain his throne. Cornwall blinds Gloucester, and the old Earl wanders towards Dover accompanied by Edgar disguised as Poor Tom. When Edgar finally abandons his disguise and reveals himself to his father, Gloucester dies of joy, and Edgar goes on to avenge himself against, and kill, his brother Edmund.

It is highly unusual for a Shakespearean tragedy to have two fully developed plots rather than a main plot and several subactions. In this case the two plots create the sense that all the play's horrors are repeated over and over, as one plot echoes the other. Blinded by selfishness and victims of their own gullibility, the two fathers suddenly embrace their selfishly calculating children, driving away Cordelia and Edgar, the offspring they once favoured. The fathers then have to live with the treachery of those with whom they have sided. Old age has made neither of these fathers wise, and their foolish actions leave their kingdom, as well as their families, in shambles. Later in this book we will compare the experiences of Lear and Gloucester and of their offspring further, and I will ask you to write about the consequences of Shakespeare's constant juxtaposition of these two strands of action. What does it do to our understanding of Lear? Of the nature of suffering? Of the actions that might rescue humanity from such suffering?

Of special importance, moreover, is that both plots begin with what would typically be the crisis of the action. Most often, a Shakespeare tragedy spends several acts introducing the audience to the characters and to the conflicts that will propel the action; then in the third act the conflicts come to a head and a decisive action occurs – the plot crisis – that sets in motion an inevitable movement towards the death of the protagonist(s) and the resolution of plot conflicts in Act 5. In *Hamlet,* for example, the protagonist spends several acts attempting to discover who murdered his father; in Act 3 he puts on a play that convinces him of the guilt of his uncle Claudius and launches Hamlet into a series of actions (the murder of Polonius, Hamlet's banishment and his return to Denmark) that conclude with Hamlet fighting a duel in which he himself dies but also murders Claudius. The play-within-the-play is the turning point or crisis of the action. By contrast, because of the love test, Lear precipitates the crisis of the plot in the first scene when in anger he banishes his youngest daughter and his loyal counsellor, Kent, and submits himself to the mercies of his elder daughters, Goneril and Regan. The consequences of that rash act roll on and on through the humiliations, assaults, madness and wandering that characterize Lear's journey until he is reunited with Cordelia. Likewise, Gloucester, in scene 2 of Act 1, is tricked into believing that his legitimate son, Edgar, plots his death, and he then puts his trust in the untrustworthy Edmund. Again, the consequences of this rash decision go on and on, culminating in Gloucester's offstage death in Act 5. This unusual management of the two plots makes the play's events feel especially harrowing and apocalyptic, so unrelieved is the suffering the play depicts and so relentless the unfolding of the consequences of the initial rash decisions that motivate each of the two plots.

It must be noted, however, that along with the terror and pity evoked by the cruel suffering of Lear and Gloucester, the persistence of kindness winds like a river through the play's action. *Kindness,* as we will see, is a complicated word, meaning both what we mainly take it to mean today, namely, feelings of fondness, affection or love for someone; good will; friendliness; and actions that express those emotions. The word, however, in Shakespeare's day could also mean kinship, a near or special relationship, and affection springing from this relationship. In short, *kindness* was seen in part to spring from *kinship.* The play forces a reader to ask: has the capacity for kindness to kin been destroyed in this play's world? A second question, perhaps a harder one, is to whom is a person kin? Is it only to blood relations? Or does an ethical or religious sense of kinship bind together all humans, whether tied by blood or not? If so, what do we owe to these fellow humans? And, perhaps, what does humanity owe to the creaturely world that surrounds it, and of which it is a part, and what does it owe to nature itself? Do humans have a special relationship with the earth they inhabit? What affection and care do they owe it? As we will see, the play invites such speculations, placing men and women, repeatedly, as journeyers on the earth, unhoused, travelling by foot or on horseback across vast distances, as surely as it places them in fixed houses and stately castles.

Language

Much of the emotional weight of this play is carried by its language, which is marked by many unusual and striking features. The monosyllables of Lear's final 'howl, howl, howl, howl' are but one of many times in which the play drives home its characters' emotions through chilling repetition as when Lear, imagining vengeance on the sons-in-law who have abused him, fantasizes silently moving close to them so that he can 'kill, kill, kill, kill, kill, kill!' (4.6.183). At other times, a series of monosyllables conveys the starkness of grief as when Lear leans over the dead body of Cordelia and asks: 'No, no, no life! / Why should a dog, a horse, a rat have life, / And thou no breath at all?' (5.3.304–6). While the play contains the kind of richly metaphoric language found elsewhere in Shakespeare, it also is marked, as here, by passages of moving simplicity almost completely lacking in metaphoric embellishment. To give another example, when Lear is finally reunited with Cordelia, he expects her to act as he has acted, and to punish him since he has given her cause to do so. She replies: 'No cause, no cause' (4.7.75), wiping away the language of command and revenge, and substituting for it a language of forgiveness and love.

When Lear is enraged, however, what issues from his mouth are curses and violent invective, the opposite of Cordelia's understated words of forgiveness. The play's language is studded with curses and invocations of the pagan gods. When his eldest daughter,

Goneril, commands Lear to dismiss fifty of his hundred knights and to curb the behaviour of the rest, Lear turns on her with fury:

> Hear, Nature, hear, dear goddess, hear:
> Suspend thy purpose if thou didst intend
> To make this creature fruitful.
> Into her womb convey sterility,
> Dry up in her the organs of increase,
> And from her derogate body never spring
> A babe to honour her. If she must teem,
> Create her child of spleen, that it may live
> And be a thwart disnatured torment to her.
> Let it stamp wrinkles in her brow of youth,
> With cadent tears fret channels in her cheeks,
> Turn all her mother's pains and benefits
> To laughter and contempt, that she may feel
> How sharper than a serpent's tooth it is
> To have a thankless child. Away, away!
>
> (1.4.267–81)

This is the first of many curses Lear visits upon his daughters. The repetition three times of the word *hear* in the first line registers Lear's impatience. He must be heard by Nature herself, here imagined as a figure with the power to punish Goneril by making her sterile or making her bring forth ungrateful and savage children. The play threads the language of Nature and the unnatural throughout its action, and at this moment Lear calls on Nature to create unnatural effects, revealing the King's own perversity. He asks Nature to make Goneril infertile, unable to perform what are typically considered the natural tasks of motherhood. Moreover, Lear's curse attempts to perpetuate an unnatural breach between parent and child into another generation. Angry at Goneril's resistance to his authority, he commands Nature, should Goneril have a child, to make it fretful, ungrateful, cruel – a perpetual torment to its mother. A long string of imperatives ties the speech together: *Hear, hear, hear, suspend, convey, dry up, create, let, turn.* The language is relentless, expressing the righteous certitude with which Lear calls down this terrible curse on his eldest daughter, refusing moderation, refusing self-scrutiny, attempting to make Nature itself man's servant.

A question raised by such language, of course, is whether it has efficacy. Goneril dies a suicide after poisoning her sister, but the audience is invited to wonder if Lear's curses determine her fate, just as it is invited to wonder if his attempts to bend the winds and the weather to his will are successful or merely an exercise in vanity. The play's juxtaposition of the towering rages and titanic curses in which Lear indulges with simple expressions of love, fidelity and forgiveness asks audiences to consider what uses of language sustain human life and community and which lead to the fracturing of bonds of kinship and care.

If Cordelia is instrumental in Lear's recovery from madness and in helping him to lay by his towering rages and desire for revenge, Lear's Fool has a different job: to force on Lear an awareness of his folly, and for this task the Fool is given a very special language of riddles, jests and puns. From the end of Act 1 to the end of Act 3, the Fool is the old King's constant companion as he journeys between the houses of his daughters and of the Earl of Gloucester and then follows Lear out into the storm. Despite his master's evident folly, the Fool is one of the play's faithful few, remaining loyal even when a 'reasonable' person would run away. In the medieval and early modern periods, fools were regular members of a king's household. Their job was to entertain the monarch, and as a result of their position they were granted a certain licence or freedom to speak irreverently and to critique the world around them. The Fool in *King Lear* has no name; he is simply Lear's Fool, and he was probably played by Robert Armin, the actor in Shakespeare's company who during the early seventeenth century took on the part of the Fool in several of Shakespeare's plays. Armin had a good singing voice, and as Lear's Fool he not only engages in witty byplay with Lear, but occasionally breaks into song or riddles. It is possible that the same actor played the parts of the Fool and of Cordelia because the two characters are never on the stage at the same time and because women's roles were played by male actors on the early modern stage. It is an attractive if unprovable idea, if only because these characters both offer Lear possibilities for self-knowledge and an exit from what he himself calls the 'wheel of fire' (4.7.47) – a wheel of hate and egotism – on which he has impaled himself.

Lear's Fool is a bitter one in the sense that he anatomizes Lear's folly ruthlessly, but often through a song, a riddle or a side comment. For example, Lear, trying to shame Goneril into recognizing his rights as her father, asks her: 'Who is it that can tell me who I am?' (1.4.221). He means for his daughter to say: 'the King, my father.' But the Fool immediately quips: 'Lear's shadow' (1.4.222). What the Fool implies is that Lear, having given away his land and his power to his two ruthless daughters, now is no longer a king or even fully in possession of his fatherly authority, but is the mere shadow of his former self. The Fool's line, only a part line, abruptly breaks the forward motion of the exchange between Lear and his daughter, the break underscoring a truth Lear should acknowledge. He can no longer command those around him because he has relinquished the power he once had. But Lear does *not* acknowledge what the Fool has said, and Goneril proceeds to further humiliate her father, proving the truth of the Fool's comment.

At another moment, Lear asks Goneril why she is frowning. The Fool breaks in: 'Thou wast a pretty fellow when thou hadst no need to care for her frowning. Now thou art an O without a figure; I am better than thou art now. I am a fool, thou art nothing' (1.4.182–5). This is a complicated passage. On one level the Fool is simply driving home the point that Lear by his own actions has changed his social position. He has lost his social identity as king but has not come to terms with that fact. Even a fool is better off than such an impotent figure because at least the Fool still has his identity as a fool. But there is also an intricate mathematical joke at work here, turning on the status of a zero. When it has a 'figure', such as a 1, a 2, or another number in front of it, the zero gains value. Instead of zero, it helps to signify 10 or 20. The 'figure' Lear has lost is his crown and kingly power. Without those, he is from one perspective just a zero, a 'nothing'.

That word, *nothing,* as we will explore further in the course of this book, is repeated at other points in the play. It raises important questions about value: what gives a person worth? What gives words value? Is flattery of more worth than understated truth? Are kings of more worth than ordinary people? Are kings of value even when they neglect their duties or behave like tyrants? The Fool's riddles, interjections and songs, because they are different from the ordinary speech of most of the play's characters, invite the audience and Lear to see and to think outside the box, to question their own assumptions about such basic things as human worth and value. When, for example, the King's faithful servant Kent is put in the stocks by Lear's older daughters, the Fool sings him a little song:

That sir which serves and seeks for gain,
And follows but for form,
Will pack when it begins to rain,
And leave thee in the storm;
But I will tarry, the Fool will stay,
And let the wise man fly:
The knave turns fool that runs away,
The fool no knave, perdy.

(2.2.267–74)

The Fool sings here of the difference between those who serve their masters for their own gain and those who serve because duty or love compel their choices. Predicting the coming storm, the Fool proclaims that he will not run away, as knaves will do, when the going gets rough. If the Fool *is* a fool, he is one in the tradition of holy fools like Christ, who gave his life to save humankind. The play is set in a pagan era, but in the actions of the Fool and Cordelia, in particular, it subtly prefigures the values of the New Testament: love and self-sacrifice.

Finally, I want to say a word about a few of the play's striking lexical features. The text abounds in the common names for an astonishing array of animals and birds: dragons, mongrels, curs, hedge sparrows, cuckoos, asses, horses, sea monsters, foxes, oysters, snails, vultures, wolves, owls, lions, cocks, lice, pelicans, hogs, dolphins, worms, sheep, civet cats, mastiffs, greyhounds, spaniels, frogs, toads, tadpoles, newts, mice, deer, vermin, nightingales, herring, tigers, crows, beetles, larks, wrens, swine, adders, butterflies, rats. In the course of this book we will inquire further into the density of these references, as well as to the many allusions to parts of the human body: eyes, arms, hands, visages, faces, hearts, legs, wombs, tongues, hair, countenances, organs of increase, nails, heels, brains, flesh, loins, blood, and more. The play repeatedly calls attention to the unstaged creatures that people the thoughts of the play's characters, enveloping the human with an imagined world of birds, beasts and sea monsters. At the same time, it repeatedly foregrounds the actual bodies of the actors who play the King, his daughters and retainers, showing their suffering by means of thorns stuck in flesh, heels placed on eyes, flesh exposed to rain and mud. The men and women of this play are bound together by a creaturely fleshiness that, despite clothing and castles, makes them all too vulnerable to

wounds and blows. In short, every aspect of *King Lear*'s language –
its riddles, curses, repetitions, iterated vocabulary, and much more –
is pregnant with potential meaning. It is only by engaging closely and
deeply with this language that we can begin to apprehend what this
play invites its audiences to feel and to think.

Structure

If careful attention to the play's language opens up its potential
meanings on a local level, as well as across different moments of the
text, in the theatre the play is held together – given dramatic shape
– by the orchestration of bodies passing before our eyes. By the time
he wrote *King Lear* in 1606, Shakespeare was a master theatrical
craftsman. He had learned to make the movement and placement of
bodies a key part of how his plays convey meaning. To take just one
example, there are three key scenes in the play in which Lear is
onstage with most of the cast onstage with him: the first courtroom
scene (1.1), the scene before Gloucester's castle (2.2), and the final
scene of the play on the battlefield at Dover (5.3). In the first scene,
King Lear is every inch a king if by that we mean a man who holds
centre stage and determines the actions of everyone else. He calls
for a map, commands his daughters to take part in the love test,
summons Burgundy and France, Cordelia's suitors, to appear before
him, banishes Kent, and dismisses Cordelia. This scene is a visual
demonstration of Lear's centrality in the world as he has known it
for eighty years: all roads lead to him, his word and his will are
absolute.

By contrast, in 2.2, Lear stands before the gates of Gloucester's
castle with a handful of retainers; his counsellor Kent is in the
stocks behind him, the Fool at his side. He is now a suppliant,
asking his daughter Regan and her husband to come out to speak
with him, asking that they grant him the respect he believes he still
deserves, asking them to allow him to retain his promised retinue of
knights. But now his daughter and son-in-law are the ones with
absolute power, and they deny his requests, allowing him to rush off
unprotected into the storm, and then shutting the castle gates to bar
his entry. The vectors of power have been completely reversed, a
reality that the old King vainly resists, despite the repeated attempts
of the Fool to get him to understand his diminished state. Lear then

sets off on his mad journey to Dover, and only once again is he surrounded by all the play's surviving figures. That is in the play's very last scene. At this point, the most notable survivors, Edgar and Goneril's husband Albany, are ready to reinvest Lear with the crown and with his former powers. But instead of resuming his position of command, Lear has eyes only for the corpse of Cordelia, vainly willing her to live. Nothing else is important to him, his old position of command utterly irrelevant.

In one sense this change in perspective perhaps shows a reorientation of values for the old King. Power is less important now than giving and receiving love and affection. And yet Lear's actions have cost him the life of his beloved daughter. This is what tragedy looks like. The protagonist has learned too late what is of value, and his mistake can never be completely undone. Moreover, because he has been a king, Lear has more than personal business to which he must attend. His actions have also stripped his kingdom of wise counsellors, now mostly dead or dying, and without a clear line of monarchical succession. The ending of Lear could not be more bleak: the stage is littered with bodies, the smoke of battle has hardly cleared, and the King dies without an heir. In many productions, it is unclear which of the surviving courtiers will be willing to pick up the mantle of kingship. This sequence of three big group scenes binds the play together, providing anchor points for the audience to see in the orchestration of bodies on the stage the gradual destruction of a kingdom and its ruling structures as well as the ever-more-frightening shattering of the protagonist's hold on power, on sanity, on the ability to keep safe what he has come to find most valuable.

Another striking example of Shakespeare's dramatic craftsmanship occurs in the structuring of Act 3, the part of the action that occurs during the wild storm on the heath after Lear has fled into the night from the gates of Gloucester's castle. The act has a dialectical structure, moving from scenes involving Lear to scenes involving events within Gloucester's castle. Lots of things happen in the outdoor scenes: Lear rages; meets Poor Tom; tries to take off his own garments to match the nakedness of this poor beggar; gradually loses his wits; takes shelter in a hovel; holds a ridiculous mock trial of his daughters; and is hastily taken, while asleep, on a litter towards Dover where his friends hope to reunite him with Cordelia. These scenes are cacophonous, shot through with claps of thunder and the howling of the wind, along with Lear's curses and imprecations, Poor Tom's mad foolery, and the Fool's increasingly plaintiff jests and songs. The world seems to be turned on its head.

Back in the castle another kind of madness erupts as Edmund, Gloucester's bastard son, informs Regan and her husband that his father Gloucester is attempting to help the old King and is in contact with Cordelia's forces. Regan and Cornwall confront Gloucester and torture him, violently gouging out his eyes and then turning him loose to wander at will. Edmund, meanwhile, commences a sexual dalliance with Goneril, which makes Regan jealous. The castle, supposedly the seat of civilized values and of shelter from storms both literal and figurative, becomes a site of torture, unbridled sexuality and the betrayal of kin. Bouncing back and forth between these exterior and interior scenes, the play batters the audience emotionally, making it seem as if there is no place of refuge for the characters or for the audience. Both must endure tortuously difficult and prolonged exposure to suffering.

At the same time, the particular dramatic structuring of Act 3 also serves a different theatrical purpose. It gives the actor playing Lear a time to rest between his two appearances on the heath in the storm and before the mock trial scene in the farmhouse. Act 3 is notoriously strenuous and demanding for the actor playing Lear, especially if the actor approaches Lear's own age of 80. Throughout the rest of this book we will examine ways in which Shakespeare both structures his play for maximum theatrical effectiveness and to accommodate the needs and highlight the skills of his acting troupe.

Sources

As with many of his plays, Shakespeare draws on prior source material for much of the action of the main plot. In this instance, he bases the play on an oft-told tale of a legendary king of ancient Britain. First recorded by Geoffrey of Monmouth in his twelfth-century *Historia Regum Britanniae* (*History of the Kings of Britain*), the received story focused on the overthrow of the aged king by his wicked daughters and their husbands. This version of the story was repeated in sixteenth-century histories, such as Raphael Holinshed's

Chronicles of England, Scotland, and Ireland and in a play written about 1594 called *The True Chronicle History of King Leir*. While there are quite a few differences between Shakespeare's version of the story and these earlier ones, the most startling innovation involves the tale's conclusion. In most earlier renditions of the Lear story, Lear recovers his kingdom with the help of Cordelia and rules until he dies a natural death. Cordelia does not die, either, but instead inherits her father's throne at his death, though after several years she commits suicide, having been deposed by her nephews. If theatregoers came to Shakespeare's tragedy with prior knowledge of the prose histories in which the story of Lear was told or with knowledge of the earlier stage play, they would have been shocked to find that Lear outlives his youngest daughter and never recovers his throne.

The bleakness of this ending has disturbed many readers, critics and audience members. After the Restoration, for example, Nahum Tate was so upset by Cordelia's death that he rewrote the ending of the play so that Lear does not die and Cordelia marries Edgar, the King of France having conveniently disappeared from the story. Other readers, such as Samuel Johnson in the eighteenth century, also could not bear to read the scene of Cordelia's death because it affected them so deeply. One question to consider is why Shakespeare made his version of the Lear story so bleak. Why does he not allow either Cordelia or King Lear to survive?

There are other important differences between Shakespeare's *Lear* and the *Leir* play of 1594. Shakespeare, for example, added Lear's madness, added the crucial character of the Fool to the main plot, and created a King notable for his irascibility. By contrast, the protagonist of *Leir* was given a milder and more patient temperament, and the play sets the story within an explicitly Christian framework. Just as importantly, Shakespeare added the second plot, that of Gloucester and his two sons, a story that he lifted from Sir Philip Sidney's prose romance, *The Arcadia*, in which a king is deposed and blinded by his illegitimate son and rescued by his good son. As I have argued, this crucial addition heightened the emotional intensity of the play as each plot's mistakes, cruel actions and immense suffering were mirrored and magnified by the presence of the other plot. The story of Edgar's disguise as Poor Tom also borrows some language from a prose pamphlet by Samuel Harsnett, *The Declaration of Egregious Popish Impostures*. In it Harsnett attacks Jesuits who, in his view, pretend to exorcize demons from those who are possessed and so con people into believing lies. Some of the demons named in the pamphlet are also named by Poor Tom in his ravings on the heath, and Poor Tom is the disguise by which Edgar deceives those around him, including his father, of his true identity. In short, many texts fed Shakespeare's imagination as he wrote this tragedy, but he combined, modified and added to those sources with remarkable creativity.

Texts

One of the most interesting facts about *King Lear* is that it exists in two different versions. While scholars do not agree on the relationship between the two, it is now widely believed, including by this scholar, that the first version of the play, called Quarto 1 (or Q1), which was printed in 1608, was probably based on the actual paper manuscript that Shakespeare himself wrote. His acting company, The King's Men, printed a number of his plays during the dramatist's lifetime in small books – quartos – for which the large sheets of paper on which plays were printed had been folded twice to produce eight pages or leaves. The size was approximately nine and a half inches by twelve. Such books were easy to carry around and slip into one's clothing. Later, when members of The King's Men wanted to collect Shakespeare's plays after his death in 1616, they added a somewhat different version of the play to the Folio edition of his works printed in 1623. For a folio text, the paper is folded only once, producing four pages or leaves of text. These were big, expensive books, approximately twelve inches by nineteen, and a folio publication signalled that a book was considered important. It was often used for publishing classical authors; Shakespeare was one of the first early modern dramatists whose collected works came out in folio form.

Interestingly, the title page of the Quarto version of the text calls it *The History of King Lear*; the Folio version calls it *The Tragedy of King Lear* and groups it with his tragedies and not with his histories such as *Henry V*. Most critics now, including myself, treat *Lear* primarily as one of Shakespeare's tragedies, but its sources, as we have seen, include historical works like Raphael Holinshed's *Chronicles of England, Scotland, and Ireland*, from which Shakespeare drew heavily in writing his many plays on late medieval English history. Calling *Lear* a history may be nothing more than a nod to the fact that the story of Lear can be found in a number of historical chronicles. But the past in this play is a pagan past before the Christianization of the British Isles occurred. In important ways the play is a thought experiment about how a culture without the benefit of Christian teachings deals with the omnipresent threats posed by ambition, greed and violence. Is such a culture more 'primitive' and lawless than seventeenth-century culture, its structures of sovereignty more fragile? To test that idea we might remember that, in November of 1605, a plot was uncovered to assassinate Britain's Protestant ruler, King James, who was on the throne when Shakespeare wrote *King Lear*. A group of conspirators placed gunpowder under the Houses of Parliament to blow up both parliament and king on the opening day of parliamentary deliberations. Though the plot was discovered before it could be executed, it was a vivid reminder of the possibility of the dangers into which a kingdom could be plunged should its ruler be killed or incapacitated. Civil war or the intrusion of foreign powers was all too possible. Shakespeare's play invites its audiences to find in the legendary 'history' of ancient Britain a way to consider present dangers as much as to call out the supposed barbarism of Britain's past.

Besides having different generic designations, *history* and *tragedy*, the Folio *King Lear* differs in many other ways from the Quarto, and scholars have struggled to account for the origin of the changes. Did Shakespeare himself revise the play, or were the changes made by someone else, possibly members of his acting company? We don't know, but what we can say is that the Folio text makes a number of cuts, especially in the last two acts, that streamline and intensify the storyline in ways consistent with effective playhouse presentation. In all, Q1 contains 300 lines that don't appear in F, while F has 100 lines that don't appear in Q. Several scenes disappear altogether in the Folio, the most significant of which is the striking scene at the end of Act 3 in which the mad Lear stages a mock trial with the Fool and Poor Tom to bring his elder daughters to justice. You may want to write about the consequences of such a change. How does it alter our understanding of Lear or of the play's examination of earthly justice and the possibility for bringing justice out of moral chaos and evil? Does the 'trial scene' so undercut the very forms and instruments of justice that the idea of justice itself is mocked, showing how it can become nothing more than a vehicle for revenge? Alternatively, does the scene create the desire for something different, a more merciful approach to human faults? Only a close examination of the scene and its language can help you decide the significance of the scene and of its excision from the Folio text.

Other, smaller changes are also important. For example, both versions of the play end with this solemn speech:

> The weight of this sad time we must obey,
> Speak what we feel, not what we ought to say.
> The oldest have borne most; we that are young
> Shall never see so much, nor live so long.

(5.3.322–5)

Consisting, like other important speeches in the play, almost entirely of monosyllables, this speech has a simplicity born of exhaustion. The speaker feels the cumulative 'weight' of the terrible suffering the play has depicted and struggles to find a way to speak what he 'feels' rather than offering clichéd words of consolation. The two couplets (pairs of lines joined by rhyme, here by the full rhyme of *obey* and *say* and the slant or partial rhyme of *young* and *long*) create a sense of an ending. Something terrible has finished, something in which the older generation carried the greatest burden of loss and suffering. After such events, what future can there be?

But who speaks these lines? In the Quarto they are delivered by Albany, Goneril's husband, who has fitfully opposed his wife's abuse of her father; in the Folio they are delivered by Edgar, the loyal son of Gloucester who accompanied his blind father to Dover in the disguise of Poor Tom. It seems possible that the person who speaks these lines is assuming de facto control of the battered kingdom. After you have read the entire play and traced the evolving characterizations of Albany and Edgar, you will be asked to consider the implications of having one or the other of these men deliver the play's final lines. Do you think that one would be the better ruler or has more claim to the throne? Are there any hints that Albany and Edgar might vie for the throne, causing the crown once more to become an object of contention? Or would you argue that neither man is eager to take up the burden of rule and that the kingdom may simply drift into chaos? What textual evidence can you adduce to support your views?

Characters, keywords, themes

Characters are important dramatic devices for drawing audiences into a play's action and so into its exploration of the themes and issues the play's language and action set forth. Shakespeare, of course, lived long before Sigmund Freud and before our current ideas about human psychology and motivation were invented. His characters are defined more through their social roles than through what we might call their 'personalities.' For example, Lear is a king and father, two social roles of immense importance in early modern England. Both kings and fathers were invested with considerable authority over the lives of their subjects and household members, but along with the power invested in these social roles came responsibilities. Kings and fathers were to provide protection, food and shelter for those under their care. In their turn, subjects and family members owed their king and father certain things: obedience, service and, often, labour. A web of interdependency and mutual obligation ideally was meant to bind together rulers and ruled, fathers and children. Things, of course, could go wrong with this idealized picture. Rulers, for example, could fail to care properly for their subjects and become tyrants; fathers could fail to care properly for their children and become *domestic* tyrants. Some political thinkers of the period worried about a subject's rights when this occurred. Could tyrants be killed, deposed or disobeyed? Could children rebel against abuse?

King Lear is not a moral or political treatise, but it raises these questions in vivid if indirect ways, partly by repeating and so calling attention to certain situations and keywords. For example, when Lear sets the love test and asks his daughters to say who loves him best, is this a request he should legitimately make? Is he fulfilling his duties as a father in the right way here? At least one of his daughters, Cordelia, apparently thinks not as she refuses to meet his demand. Why does she do this? In answering, you will want to do more than speculate about Cordelia's personality; instead, we will look at the language Cordelia uses in replying to her father since it is largely language that *creates* what we understand her character to be. Specifically, when Cordelia says, 'I love your majesty / According to my bond, no more nor less' (1.1.92–3), what does she mean? Using the *Oxford English Dictionary* to explore the period's definition of *bond* is a place to start, along with carefully examining the other statements Cordelia makes during her encounter with her father. Does she have socially justified reasons for refusing his request, or is she simply failing her duties as a daughter? At the same time, consider the language her sisters use in replying to their father. How would you characterize the language with which they answer Lear? What do their words reveal about their understanding of their social bonds to those around them?

Servant is another key word of importance to *Lear*, and you might use Martin Spevak's *The Harvard Concordance to Shakespeare*, or search an online version of the text of *King Lear*, to see just how often the word is used in the play. Servants are not necessarily people of low birth or rank in the early modern period. They could be an earl, like Kent, who holds a privileged position as servant and wise counsellor to the King, or they could be slippery fellows like Oswald, who serves as a steward in Goneril's household, or the lowly unnamed servants in Cornwall's household who attempt to stop him from gouging out Gloucester's eyes. What are the duties of servants? When should they obey, and when, if ever, should they not obey their masters? What do the repeated events involving servants in this play invite the audience to think about these questions as when, for example, Kent blatantly disobeys the King's commands in the play's first scene and is banished as a result. What language does Kent use in his act of defiance, and what language does Lear use in response? Who is in the right? What clash of values is enacted in their exchange?

In what follows, we will return to many of the ideas and topics briefly sketched in this introduction, using various research and writing exercises to unpack *King Lear*'s many potential meanings. Attention to language can take us deeper into all the issues we have identified, especially when we also come to recognize that there is a language of props and costumes, such as maps and handkerchiefs, that the early modern stage employed, along with words, to convey meaning to audience members. Consequently, we will examine the meaning-making function of these physical objects as well as the many unique linguistic features of this tragedy as we investigate how the many languages of the stage operate. There is much to explore, so let's get going.

CHAPTER ONE

Language

From Words to Embodied Speaking

Preliminaries

Drama is a special art form in that it can be read in a book or performed on a stage. When a play is read aloud or fully staged, meaning derives both from the semantic content of speech and also from the sound of the spoken words. In this chapter we are going to explore the language of *King Lear* at the local level of the single word, the poetic line, the speech, and brief exchanges between two characters. As we do, we will pay attention to how language works in each of these units, attending both to sound and to sense. For example, when King Lear first rushes out into the storm in the second scene of Act 3, he cries: 'Blow winds and crack your cheeks! Rage, blow!' (3.2.1). There is much to say about this one line. First, the old king is giving orders to the natural world. He uses imperative verb forms, commanding the winds to *blow*, *crack*, and *rage*, showing that it is in his character to assume he can order the world to conform to his desires. Just as he once gave commands to his daughters and servants, he now tries to do the same to the winds. But is he really in charge of the elements, or is he living in a fantasy world? Moreover, those one-syllable imperative verbs invite the actor playing Lear to spit them out, expelling anger with every exhalation of breath. Raging, Lear commands the elements to rage, confusing his own emotion with what he wants to believe the storm is expressing. Some of Lear's words here, like *crack*, sound like what they mean, in this case the noise of something breaking or being rent apart. This is an example of *onomatopoeia*, that is, the use of a word, the sound of which suggests its meaning. The effect of Lear's line is thus created by a number of factors: the driving repetition of imperative verbs, the semantic force of words like *rage* and *blow*, and the explosive sound of words like *crack*. In everything that follows in this chapter we will attend to how words mean as part of an implicit performative act in which meaning grows from the fusion of speech, sound, and the wordless language of the body. Many of our examples will be taken from the crucial first scene of the play.

Before we turn to an in-depth exploration of words, lines and speeches, however, I want to do some preliminary work having to do with how words in a play 'look' when we read them on the page. Much information is conveyed by capitalized words, words set off in italics or brackets, words organized in the patterned forms of poetry or the continuous word blocks of prose. In this first section we will take up how printed play texts display words in distinctive ways so that we can better understand how to read a play to absorb all the information it conveys and the special effects it creates.

When we read Shakespeare's plays, we quickly learn that nearly all of them – and *Lear* is no exception – are written in a mixture of prose and poetry. Poetry has a distinctive rhythm, sometimes employs rhyme, and often has a set and recurring number of syllables in each line. Shakespeare typically wrote the verse parts of his plays in iambic pentameter, that is, in lines that each have five metrical feet, each foot having an unaccented syllable followed by an accented syllable. A perfect iambic pentameter line feels in our heads like ba-boom, ba-boom, ba-boom, ba-boom, ba-boom. For example, in one of Lear's first speeches in Act 1 he speaks a perfectly regular iambic pentameter line: 'Since now we will divest us both of rule' (1.1.49). The accented syllables are *now, will, vest, both* and *rule*. Shakespeare used the iambic pentameter line with great regularity, but he did not follow its dictates slavishly. Instead, as we will explore below, he often varied the rhythm and number of syllables in each line to produce special effects and to give the illusion that his characters were speaking spontaneously.

In most of Shakespeare's plays, verse is spoken by high-ranking figures or used in scenes where important business is conducted. Typically, Shakespeare does not often use end rhyme – that is, rhymes created by the final word of one line chiming with the final word of another line – except at the conclusion of scenes or arcs of action when rhyme marks the moment when the stage is about to empty or another action is about to begin. For example, after Lear has banished Kent, his faithful counsellor, Kent says:

> Why, fare thee well, King, since thus thou wilt appear,
> Freedom lives hence and banishment is here.
> [*to Cordelia*] The Gods to their dear shelter take thee, maid,
> That justly think'st and hast most rightly said;
> [*To Goneril and Regan*] And your large speeches may your
>   deeds approve,
> That good effects may spring from words of love,
> Thus Kent, O princes, bids you all adieu;
> He'll shape his old course in a country new.
>   (1.1.181–8)

Kent is about to disappear from the court; he bids a formal farewell to those he is leaving, addressing his old master first, then the king's youngest daughter, then the two elder sisters, and finally the other 'princes' assembled around Lear. Kent speaks to each using a rhymed couplet or pair of adjoining rhymed lines. The rhyme sets his words off from the surrounding dialogue. It marks the end of something important: Kent's publicly acknowledged service to his king before a new action begins with the arrival of Cordelia's suitors, the King of France and the Duke of Burgundy. When we next see Kent, he will be disguised as a common serving man, still loyal to his master, but not recognized by him.

We might also note that much of his speech employs regular iambic pentameter, befitting Kent's dignified and controlled response to his involuntary dismissal from court. But metrical irregularities do enter his speech. See, for example, how, in the first line, the word *King* has unusual prominence, standing alone, separating the line's first two metrical feet from the final three. This unusual extra foot allows Kent to put an ironic emphasis on the word, calling subtle attention to the fact that Lear has not been acting like a king but like a wilful tyrant. Note also that the second line contains two metrically irregular feet. The first foot, consisting of the word *freedom*, is a trochaic foot, that is, it puts the accent on the first syllable, followed by an unstressed syllable, thus reversing the pattern found in iambic pentameter. The second foot, consisting of the words *lives hence*, has two equally stressed syllables, and is called a spondee. Together, these two breaks with the metrical regularity of much of the rest of the speech force the actor saying these lines to slow down, thus calling attention to the terrible indictment he is laying at Lear's feet: 'Freedom lives hence.' No one in Lear's kingdom is truly free, especially not free to speak the truth.

By contrast, prose is most often employed in scenes involving ordinary people, those who do not hold an elevated class position. It is also common in scenes of jest and fooling and in those in which figures conduct mundane business. Shakespearean prose can employ complex or straightforward sentence structures, but it does not have metre, a set line length, or rhyme. You will notice that the first words of *King Lear* are written in prose. Two of Lear's counsellors, the Earl of Kent and the Earl of Gloucester, are speaking together in the presence of Gloucester's illegitimate son, Edmund. Kent says: 'I thought the King had more affected the Duke of Albany than Cornwall,' to which Gloucester replies: 'It did always seem so to us: but now, in the division of the kingdom, it appears not which of the dukes he values most, for qualities are so weighed that curiosity in neither can make choice of either's moiety' (1.1–6). In other words, Lear has divided his kingdom so equitably that no one knows which son-in-law he favours.

It is curious why Kent and Gloucester are given prose in this scene. Both men are high-ranking officials in Lear's court, not ordinary people. They begin by talking about state business, namely, whom the old King favours as he is about to step down from his role as an active monarch. They then turn to discussing Edmund, why Kent has never met him, and why Edmund will not remain long in England.

Why do you think this speech is written in prose? It may be because the two older men are primarily gossiping, speaking informally and privately, both about affairs of state and about Gloucester's family. As it will turn out, the anger that Edmund feels at being illegitimate, and so not in line to be his father's heir, will be a powerful motivating force in Edmund's actions later in the play. In retrospect, then, we can see irony in the casual way in which Gloucester jests about his son's birth and social position in this scene. The Earl's casualness, signalled by his use of prose, will come back to haunt him when Edmund later takes his revenge. In the same way, the men's casual talk about the division of the kingdom does not anticipate the furious rage the issue unleashes when Lear attaches it to the so-called 'love test' in which his daughters are asked to compete for his affection before getting their 'share' of the kingdom. It is as if within one scene the play accelerates in emotional intensity from 5 miles an hour to 80 with very little transition.

The crucial division of the words of *King Lear* into prose and poetry is, however, only one of the ways the presentation of language on the page conveys information. We know, for example, by the way some words in modern printed play texts are set off in capital letters that they are not spoken by any character. Instead, they are included in the printed text to let readers know who speaks particular lines. These capitalized words are called 'speech prefixes'. In performance, there is no need for such information as the audience can clearly see who is speaking and hear the different vocal tones of the actors playing each role. Many speech prefixes are proper names, like LEAR or KENT. Sometimes, the speech prefix will only describe a person's social role as in FOOL or SERVANT I. This is a reminder that in the early modern period a person's individuality was often subordinated to their position in society.

King Lear also contains a number of words that are printed in a distinctive typeface, namely, italics; these are also set off from the spoken dialogue. These italicized words are called 'stage directions'. They sometimes contain the proper names of characters, by convention printed in capital letters. For example, before Kent speaks the first words of the play, a reader will see the following words: '*Enter* KENT, GLOUCESTER *and* EDMUND.' This stage direction tells actors to perform a certain action. Here that action is an entrance. Sometimes a stage direction will indicate a sound or special effect that would be created by offstage theatre personnel. For example, in the third act of *Lear*, the stage direction *Storm still* appears several times (see, for example, the stage direction before 3.2). We know that early modern theatres had 'thunder sheets', that is, pieces of metal that could be shaken to create the effect of thunder. Probably these thunder sheets were used liberally throughout this part of the play. In performance, stage directions are not spoken, but they are necessary if readers are to understand the implicit soundscape of a play when they are not actually attending a production of it.

As you read *King Lear*, be attentive to three kinds of stage directions: original stage directions, later stage directions added by editors, and implied stage directions. Original stage directions are those contained in the first printed editions of a play. As we learned in the Introduction to this book, for *King Lear* those first printed editions are the First Quarto of 1608 and the Folio of 1623. Both stage directions discussed in the prior paragraph are original in the sense that they appear in one of those two texts of the play. However, later editors frequently added stage directions not found in the first printed texts in order to clarify important events in the action, such as when entrances or exits occur or when a sound effect should be heard. These stage directions are printed in brackets [ ] in order to indicate that they do not appear in the first printed texts. Every edition of a Shakespeare play has slightly different stage directions added by the editor. This book draws its textual quotations from, and refers to the stage directions included in, the third series edition of the Arden Shakespeare *King Lear*. You may find some of the stage directions will be different in your edition of the play if you are not using the Arden text. This by itself is interesting and shows the interpretive powers editors have.

For example, in the first scene of *King Lear*, Cordelia listens intently to what her sisters reply when Lear asks each daughter to say how much she loves him. Before she makes her own response, however, Cordelia speaks several lines that have an ambiguous addressee. For example, at line 62, after Goneril has fulsomely attested to her love for her father, in the Arden edition of the play the speech prefix, stage direction and first line read: 'CORDELIA [*aside*]. What shall Cordelia speak? Love and be silent.' The stage direction '[*aside*]' tells a reader that Cordelia is directing her speech out towards an offstage audience, rather than towards the other onstage characters. Placed in brackets, this stage direction has been inserted by the Arden editor to indicate that no one hears these words except the audience as Cordelia ponders how to respond to the flood of insincere praise issuing from her sisters' lips. The line also makes clear Cordelia's yoking together of love and silence. Goneril and Regan speak at length about their supposed love for their father, a love that will not prove true when tested, but Cordelia decides not to follow suit and enter this empty competition. The added stage direction, [*aside*], shows her turning aside from a direct reply to the King and speaking her thoughts to herself, and to us. An interesting exercise when reading stage directions is to note which ones are placed in brackets and to decide if you think they are necessary. Are there other places in the text where you think an additional stage direction would be helpful? These plays are living documents changed every time they are performed or edited. Feel free to consider what stage directions you would add or subtract.

A final kind of stage direction does not appear in the text at all but can be assumed from the words spoken by the characters. For example, when Lear is first onstage, he immediately calls for a map so he can show how he intends to divide his kingdom among his three daughters. He says: 'Give me the map here. Know that we have divided / In three our kingdom' (1.1.36–7). In the original texts no stage direction accompanies these lines, but they clearly point to a physical action that is happening onstage. Someone, maybe Kent, maybe a servant, brings a map to the old King. Is it a rolled-up scroll that the King then unfurls on the floor? Is it laid across a table? Is it perhaps already set up on a stand and merely pulled or carried to centre stage? Directors must decide these details, but it is clear that some specific action is occurring to which the words spoken by Lear give us a clue, and you as a reader get to imagine exactly what that action should be.

Words

We have been considering how Shakespearean texts display words on a page in ways that convey meaning. Poetry and prose, stage directions and speech prefixes, and even brackets all tell attentive readers something about the meaning of the words before them. But now let's turn to the words set in ordinary typeface within the play's dialogue. As we have already begun to see, Shakespeare's dramatic language is always overcharged with meaning. Often this comes from its richly figurative nature – that is, Shakespeare's use of metaphor, simile, puns and many other devices that give his words more than one meaning or create more than one effect. This is a topic we will take up in the next chapter. But for the moment let's focus simply on the way Shakespeare highlights meaning through simple verbal repetition. In being repeated, particular words gather depth and resonance and sometimes mystery. Why does a word keep reappearing? Is it a kind of keyword, a verbal hotspot that points to a central problem that the play approaches and reapproaches? We have already touched on one such word in the first scene: *love*. Modern critics have implicitly recognized the importance of this word by naming as 'the love test' that portion of scene 1 in which Lear demands that his daughters tell him how much they love him in order to gain a portion of his kingdom. Lear throws down the challenge when he says to them: 'Which of you shall we say doth love us most?' (1.1.51). He then turns to each for an answer.

In her response, Goneril four times in seven lines evokes the word *love* or *lov'd*. Cordelia, in the aside already discussed, says she loves Lear but will not express that love in words. Regan then uses the word twice in eight lines. The irony, of course, is that while Goneril and Regan are attempting to quantify how much love they have for their father, they fail to define what that love means, in what is consists. Only Cordelia undertakes to do so when, after her initial refusal to say how much she loves her father, she finally answers him, not by competing with her sisters in exaggerated protestations of love, but by describing the reasons *why* love is owed and given. Her reply focuses on the fact that love is intricately bound up in the dense network of obligations and relations that make up human society. To her father she says:

> Good, my lord,
> You have begot me, bred me, loved me. I
> Return those duties back as are right fit,
> Obey you, love you and most honour you.
> Why have my sisters husbands, if they say
> They love you all? Haply when I shall wed,
> That lord whose hand must take my plight shall carry
> Half my love with him, half my care and duty.
> Sure I shall never marry like my sisters
> To love my father all.

> (1.1.95–104)

What do these lines tell us about what love means to Cordelia? Nowhere does she say that she does not love her father. Instead, she talks about the mutual obligations and bonds of love that tether them to one another. As he has begotten, bred and loved her, she in turn, as a matter of duty and reciprocal obligation, obeys, loves and honours him. The balanced effect of the second and fourth lines (*begot*, *bred*, *loved* juxtaposed to *obey*, *love*, *honour*) is an example of *isocolon*, the use of phrases of equal length and comparable structure. This highly patterned language by itself suggests the reciprocal relationship in which Cordelia sees herself and her father engaged. Their mutual and balanced obligations are what hold society together, keeping it from becoming merely a selfish competition among individuals, each greedy for power at others' expense. Moreover, Cordelia argues that the bonds of loving obligation are not limited to the father–child dyad. She will in the future be bound to a husband, too.

Kent is the only character who seems instinctively to understand what Cordelia is saying, partly because he has the same fidelity to the reciprocal bonds that in his world view, and Cordelia's, tie society together. He uses the word *love* in the following context. As he tries to prevent Lear from banishing Cordelia, he says: 'Royal Lear / Whom I have ever honoured as my king, / Loved as my father, as my master followed, / As my great patron thought on in my prayers –' (1.1.140–3). Here Kent, again using isocolon, names all the ways that he is bound to Lear. Lear is his king, his metaphorical father, his master, his patron. Each of those bonds demands something of him: honour, love, service, prayer. His actions flow from those commitments and obligations, including the act of love that leads him to follow Lear in the disguise of a poor man.

The repetition of the simple word *love* in this early scene thus sets up questions that the reader or spectator will follow throughout the rest of the play. Who besides Cordelia is capable of understanding and embodying a non-selfish love? Or is there some selfishness in her withholding the words Lear longs to hear? Is her love tainted by pride? Should she simply humour the old man's demands? Does Cordelia continue to display love for her father, and a sense of duty towards him, even after he has banished her? Are there other characters in the play, besides Lear, who display a selfish disregard for the obligations of love? Does Lear himself ever come to understand the shallow nature of his own original understanding of love and embrace a more complex understanding of it, or does that remain beyond him? The first scene's repetition of a single simple word thus opens up questions that will only grow more complex in their ramifications as the play unfolds.

Another keyword in scene 1 is the imperative, *speak*. Lear uses it frequently, starting at line 54 when he commands that Goneril 'speak first' about her love for him. He later makes the same demand of Regan and twice of Cordelia. As we have already noted, Lear is given to speaking in imperatives. He commands rather than asks. But this command is for something very particular: it is for speech. Ordinarily we think of speech as a good thing. We urge people to find their voices, to express themselves, to overcome trauma by naming it for what it is. These are often positive actions. In the early modern period, however, the power of human speech was both celebrated and feared. Rhetorical manuals taught people how to use language to make forceful arguments and to persuade others of their point of view. Powerful preaching was seen as a way to bring people to God; good courtroom oratory was seen as a way to advance justice and equity. But rhetorical treatises also warned that language could be used to deceive people, to persuade them of untruths, to sugarcoat lies with rhetorical 'flowers' and ornaments. Cordelia, for example, clearly feels that her sisters are using rhetoric to deceive their father by making overblown and empty promises of love. By contrast, she decides to say 'nothing' to his demands (1.1.87). A little later she relents and makes the speech discussed above in which she carefully sets forth the nature of her love, its limits, its place in a network of overlapping obligations.

Cordelia's response, and her aversion to her sister's rhetorical displays, raises the question of whether the demand to 'speak' is an invitation that should always be taken up; moreover, should speech, whenever it is rendered, be accepted at face value? Lear demands speech, but despite his eighty years of living, he seems extremely naive about the possibility of verbal deception. What his older daughters say, because it chimes with what he wants to hear, seems like truth to him. What Cordelia says, not fitting his desires, simply cannot be heard in the sense of taken in, understood, evaluated on its own terms.

Lear's demand for speech raises another issue. If elaborate speech can be deceptive, is plainness better than ornament, less speech better than more, silence the best of all? Are actions a better way to judge loyalty, say, or love, than verbal protestations? Drama is, of course, a verbal medium. All the characters, even Cordelia, use words to express their meanings, but you might want to take note of how actions speak in this play, whether it is Cornwall's gouging out of Gloucester's eyes, Cordelia's return from France to help her aged father, or the Fool's long trek behind Lear in the storm. You might also ask if there are moments when ornate speech gives way to plain speech, or almost to no speech at all. Lear's waking up from his prolonged period of madness is one such moment. See if you can identify others. Lear's demand that his daughters 'speak' underscores another of those keywords that opens the door to questions crucial to the many meanings this tragedy enacts.

Before leaving our focus on individual words, I would like to raise a final fact: words have more than one meaning. This is obvious, and yet it is extremely important to how the language of *Lear*, or the language of any of Shakespeare's plays, works. Shakespeare is a master at activating multiple meanings of a single word so that their implications just keep unfolding or are held in some kind of productive tension. A good tool, mentioned in the Introduction to this book, to help you explore the multiple meanings of words in Shakespeare's day is the *Oxford English Dictionary*. Many libraries have it online. It enables a reader to see what meaning words had in earlier centuries and so to find out many of the possible things a word could have meant in Shakespeare's day. If a word seems especially important or especially puzzling to you, this is a good place to begin to track the different things it could have meant to the dramatist.

Several words found near the very beginning of the play will briefly illustrate the ways in which Shakespeare capitalizes on the multivalent meanings of a single word. Speaking with Kent, Gloucester explains his relation to Edmund:

GLOUCESTER   His breeding, sir, hath been at my charge. I have so often blushed to acknowledge him that now I am brazed to't.

KENT   I cannot conceive you.

GLOUCESTER   Sir, this young fellow's mother could; whereupon she grew round-wombed, and had, indeed, sir, a son for her cradle ere she had a husband for her bed. Do you smell a fault?

(1.1.8–15)

The words I will focus on here are *breeding* and *conceive*. Edmund's breeding can mean both the processes of conception that led to his birth and the effort that went into raising him. Gloucester has been responsible for both a carnal act, impregnating Edmund's mother, and then paying for the upbringing of the child that resulted. But the *Oxford English Dictionary* also makes clear that the word *breeding* is often used of beasts and birds as well as of humans. This may contribute to a certain queasiness that the exchange has often produced in readers. Gloucester is talking about his illegitimate son's unlawful conception when that son is standing right beside him. It is almost as if Edmund were an animal without the ability to understand human speech and his conception not unlike the breeding of cattle. The doubleness encoded in the word *breeding* invites the reader or listener to consider what it means that Gloucester's language conjoins livestock and people. While the play will eventually invite readers to consider whether human beings are really superior to the animal world, at this point it does not so much seem to be engaging that issue as brushing aside the seriousness of Gloucester's son's out-of-wedlock conception and the effects on Edmund of his bastard status.

The same is true of the word *conceive*. Kent says he cannot conceive Gloucester, meaning he cannot understand him. Gloucester then repeats the word, but it now has a different meaning, one closer to *become pregnant*. He insinuates that Edmund's mother understood him in a sexual sense and became pregnant as a result. Gloucester's play on the word *conceive* constitutes a *pun*, that is, the use of a word to suggest two or more meanings or associations. A pun can produce a humorous effect, as it does here, when the meaning of *conceive* as *understanding* is suddenly displaced by a sexual innuendo. Gloucester's linguistic play on *conceive* can be seen as boasting about, or at least calling attention to, his sexual past. He knows the conception of Edmund involved a fault, but he discloses it as something like a joke. Again, this is done while Edmund stands beside him. The casualness with which Gloucester tells this story, the oscillation between sexual boasting and shame – shame that motivates Gloucester's intention to send Edmund out of the country again – suggests that Gloucester has not yet fully come to terms with the act of 'breeding' that led to the illegitimate 'conceiving' of his younger son and what effect his present narration of that act might have on that son.

Lines and speeches

As you can see, discussing individual words is hard to separate from discussing the lines in which they are embedded, but now I want more deliberately to take up some of the strategies Shakespeare used in creating entire speeches for his characters to say. The speech is a variable unit. It does not have a predetermined length; it can be spoken in prose or verse; it reveals something about the character of the person who speaks it, but it can do more. It can change the mood of a scene, articulate ideas important to the play as a whole, or do all of the above at once. We are now going to look at two important speeches from early in the play, both in poetry, to discuss how their language works. The first is the seven-line speech in which Goneril responds to her father's demand that she 'speak first' (1.1.54) and say how much she loves him:

> Sir, I do love you more than word can wield the matter,
> Dearer than eyesight, space and liberty,
> Beyond what can be valued, rich or rare,
> No less than life, with grace, health, beauty, honour.
> As much as child e'er loved, or father found,
> A love that makes breath poor and speech unable,
> Beyond all manner of so much I love you.

(1.1.55–61)

If you had to name the most striking aspect of this speech, what would it be? One of my students once said: 'It's a list, and kind of random.' I think that was a good answer. There *is* a list-like quality to this speech. Goneril begins and ends by saying that no words can express her love, yet paradoxically her speech attempts to do just that by listing one thing after another that Goneril values, while insisting that she loves Lear 'more', 'beyond' how she loves those things. Her eyesight, her health, life and liberty – she claims to love her father more than any of them.

The list feels both random and clichéd because each line simply repeats a basic theme, and many other valuable things could be substituted for those Goneril has hit upon. The speech ends up being hyperbolic without being specific about any of the old King's attributes or about the nature of the father–daughter relationship that would evoke such love. Compare, in this regard, Cordelia's speech about the bonds that tie her to her father. Goneril's speech does not characterize the quality of her love beyond its immensity; it aims at claiming a prize by acts of hyperbolic quantification: *more, beyond, dearer*. To be fair, Goneril is responding to a demand: tell me how much you love me. Her speech is formulaic and hyperbolic because that is what Lear's question invites. She speaks formally, in balanced phrases ('rich or rare', 'makes breath poor and speech unable'), but without energy or originality.

By contrast, consider the speech that opens the second scene of the play. The speaker is Edmund, bastard son of Gloucester, who in the first scene was the object of his father's casual jests, spoken about but hardly speaking. Here, his language fairly bursts with energy. Alone on the stage, he addresses the goddess Nature, but speaks directly to the audience, letting us in on his plans and his unorthodox values. This voice is startlingly original:

> Thou, Nature, art my goddess; to thy law
> My services are bound. Wherefore should I
> Stand in the plague of custom, and permit
> The curiosity of nations to deprive me?
> For that I am some twelve or fourteen moonshines
> Lag of a brother? Why bastard? Wherefore base?
> When my dimensions are as well compact,
> My mind as generous and my shape as true
> As honest madam's issue? Why brand they us
> With base? With baseness, bastardy? 'Base, base?'
> Who in the lusty stealth of nature take
> More composition and fierce quality
> Than doth within a dull stale tired bed
> Go to the creating of a whole tribe of fops
> Got 'tween a sleep and wake. Well, then,
> Legitimate Edgar, I must have your land.
> Our father's love is to the bastard Edmund
> As to the legitimate. Fine word, 'legitimate'!
> Well, my legitimate, if this letter speed
> And my invention thrive, Edmund the base
> Shall top the legitimate. I grow, I prosper:
> Now gods, stand up for bastards!

(1.2.1–22)

If you quickly read this passage through, what might strike you first is the speed with which it unfolds. This is partly because so many of the lines have no punctuation at the end of them (see, for example, the first three lines of Edmund's speech). This is called *enjambment*; it occurs when a sentence continues without a pause at the end of a poetic line. Repeatedly Edmund reaches the end of a line and keeps on going. This creates the impression that he is a man in a hurry, and unstoppable.

What might next strike you about this speech is the way it is laced with repetition. The repetition involves both recurring rhetorical features, like questions, and recurring keywords, like *base*, *bastard* and *legitimate*. Edmund begins by asking questions, many of them rhetorical, that is, questions to which he probably already knows the answer, but the recitation of which works Edmund up into a frenzy. 'Why bastard?' 'Wherefore base?' These questions clearly touch on the old wound so casually brought up by his father's jesting remarks to Kent. Why am I not as good as my 'legitimate' brother Edgar? Why should mere custom dictate that children born within wedlock have more rights than children born outside it? Why am I called base when I am as good as my brother in shape and wit? The questions express Edmund's resentment against the settled ways of the world; the repetition of *base* and *legitimate* makes the reader think about this binary. Why should the base son be scorned and the legitimate son exalted? Does anything important separate them? Dwelling on *base* not only plays with its association with *bastard* (illegitimate) but with other meanings of the word: *low-born*, *despicable*, *inferior*, *cowardly*. The speech becomes a cry against all the vile meanings attached to the idea of baseness. At several points Edmund invites us to re-evaluate baseness, to associate the base-born with shapely forms and active natures and to associate the legitimately born with foppishness and lack of energy since the former was conceived with genuine passion, the latter with dutiful exertion.

It is also important to note that the first part of the speech is addressed to Nature, the goddess Edmund claims as his own, a deity here opposed to the supposedly civilizing forces of custom and law and embodying something like the primal and lawless energies of the natural world. At line 15, however, Edmund begins to address his brother Edgar *in absentia*, repeatedly spitting out the word *legitimate* to characterize his brother until it seems a term of contempt. It is at this point that Edmund drops his questions and begins to outline a plan for seizing his brother's land and his privileged place as the legitimate heir. The speech ends with a rousing display of Edmund's resilience and a counter-intuitive plea for the gods to favour bastards: 'I grow, I prosper: / Now gods, stand up for bastards!'

This truly marvellous speech, in the hands of a good actor, brings the house down and temporarily, at least, draws the audience to Edmund's side. The pleasure it gives is only intensified by the suspense created by the striking use of a prop – a letter that Edmund holds throughout the speech. The opening stage direction, a mixture of original and later editorial additions, reads: '*Enter* [EDMUND, *the*] *Bastard* [, *holding a letter*].' The letter's purpose is at this point unclear, but its existence teases us. Why is Edmund holding this letter while he speaks? What is it for? Even when he directly calls attention to the paper at the end of the speech, we are only informed that it will be used in a way that will undermine Edgar, but we are not told its actual contents. We are thus plunged into the rest of the scene knowing that a mystery is still to be revealed.

In writing the speech, I like to think Shakespeare was having a lot of fun. He was also making use of the stage tradition of the Vice, a figure from medieval drama that represented the evil that Christians had to abjure, sins such as pride, gluttony and deceit. This figure, despite its associations with vice, crime and immorality, was also often the wittiest character onstage. Moreover, the Vice frequently spoke directly to the audience, taking them into his confidence. He thus embodied the allurements of sin, what made sin seductive, even as his defeat by the forces of good was the point of the action. In a loose way, Edmund draws on the Vice tradition, especially in the early scenes of the play when his wit, his daring, his iconoclasm and his vibrant speech are all a central part of his characterization. In studying this speech carefully, you can see how cleverly Shakespeare has used language to make it effective.

Before we end this discussion of the micro-units of drama (word, line and speech), I want also to take up the question of how we might attend to the special uses of language in dialogue situations, that is, when two or more speakers are talking together. Every bit of dialogue has its own internal dynamics, but I want to look at part of an exchange between Kent and Lear, again in the play's first scene. This is an important encounter in part because Kent speaks to Lear in an unexpected way, a way very different from how most other characters have addressed him publicly. It is also interesting because each character in the exchange is fully attentive to the words of the other, and their assertions and replies take on the thrust-and-parry quality of combat. Let's begin in the middle of their encounter:

KENT   What wouldst thou do, old man?
Think'st thou that duty shall have dread to speak,
When power to flattery bows? To plainness honour's bound
When majesty falls to folly. Reserve thy state,
And in thy best consideration check
This hideous rashness. Answer my life my judgement,
Thy youngest daughter does not love thee least,
Nor are those empty-hearted, whose low sounds
Reverb no hollowness.
LEAR   Kent, on thy life, no more.
KENT
My life I never held but as a pawn
To wage against thine enemies, ne'er fear to lose it,
Thy safety being the motive.
LEAR   Out of my sight!
KENT
See better Lear, and let me still remain
The true blank of thine eye.
LEAR
Now by Apollo –
KENT   Now by Apollo, King,
Thou swear'st thy gods in vain.
LEAR   O vassal! Miscreant!
ALBANY, CORNWALL   Dear sir, forbear!
KENT
So, kill thy physician, and thy fee bestow
Upon the foul disease. Revoke thy gift,
Or while I can vent clamour from my throat,
I'll tell thee thou dost evil.
LEAR Hear me, recreant, on thine allegiance, hear me.

(1.1.147–68)

Among the things one might note about the language of this angry exchange are, first, the plain unflattering diction with which Kent addresses his king. He calls him 'old man', says he has given way to 'hideous rashness', and bluntly declares: 'thou dost evil.' After the flattering tones in which others have addressed Lear, Kent's speech seems to represent a breach of decorum. How does Kent dare to treat Lear so disrespectfully? Compounding this seeming breach of etiquette are the imperatives Kent uses in addressing Lear. We have earlier noted the King's tendency to adopt the imperative mode in dealing with others, but here Kent says: 'Reserve thy state' (150) (that is, keep your power and don't give it to your daughters); 'check this hideous rashness' (151–2); 'See better Lear' (159); 'Kill thy physician' (164); 'Revoke thy gift' (165) (that is, the gift of the crown given to his heirs). In every instance, Kent is ordering Lear to do something. Lear's imperatives, 'Hear me, recreant' (168), are countered by Kent's 'See better Lear' (159). Again, how does Kent dare to give Lear orders?

The audacity of Kent and the intimate intertwining of his speech acts with Lear's are reflected in the fact that they often share a line of verse. At line 155, the King starts speaking when Kent has spoken only half a line. At line 158 he again interrupts Kent to order him: 'Out of my sight!' But when Lear starts to curse Kent in the name of Apollo, Kent interrupts him in the middle of line 161, saying he calls on Apollo in vain. This pattern of line-sharing is interesting, indicating, perhaps, the old, now highly charged, relationship between them. Each is, literally, in the other's face, interrupting the other's speeches. Lear would probably not endure rebuke from any other man as long as he endures it from Kent. Kent would probably not venture to speak as he does did not his long history of service bind the two of them together. Some of Kent's word choices indicate how he sees his duty at this moment. *Duty*, in fact, is a word he uses at line 148 to explain why he speaks when he sees Lear bowing to flattery. *Honour* is another word he evokes (149) to justify his plain speaking as he sees Lear falling to folly. Later he speaks of trying to preserve Lear's *safety* (158); still later he calls himself, in effect, Lear's *physician* (164). From these linguistic clues one can piece together Kent's understanding of his job as one of Lear's chief servants and advisors. He is to speak truth, rather than flattery, to his king in order to act like a good physician, heal Lear's folly, and preserve his safety. This is a duty he takes so seriously that even when he is banished, he returns in disguise to continue in the role. The extremity of his exchange with Lear, the degree to which he risks the King's wrath, is a measure of the danger he sees lying in wait for the King as a result of his rash actions. Do you feel it is also a sign of Kent's own intemperance? Is he a flawed counsellor or a good one? Would other speech acts have been more effective?

The languages of the body

So far in this chapter we have been talking about verbal language; in this next section we are going to talk about non-verbal language: gestures, bodily movements, the tableaux created by bodies assuming iconic or particularly striking postures. When you read a play, you have to imagine these embodied cues and be attentive to how they are signalled in the text; in performance, obviously, embodied language speaks to us directly. So what do I mean by 'embodied language'? Let me give a concrete example. Kneeling was a bodily gesture of considerable significance in early modern culture. Kneeling showed respect to someone of high status or invested with institutional significance. Priests knelt before the altar in Catholic churches to show their respect for God the Father and his Son, Jesus; nobles knelt before their king to show their allegiance; children knelt before their parents to receive their blessing. In the opening scene of *King Lear*, many editors and directors believe that Goneril and Regan both might kneel before Lear when they make their protestations of how much they love him, even though there is no explicit stage direction indicating that they are to do so. Similarly, when a furious Lear commands Kent to 'Hear me, recreant, on thine allegiance, hear me' (1.1.168), many directors have Kent kneel to receive his sentence of banishment. Kent may quarrel vigorously with Lear, but in the end he accepts Lear's authority over him.

Towards the conclusion of the play, when the old King awakens from his madness in the presence of Cordelia, editors traditionally add a direction indicating that Cordelia kneels when she asks for his blessing and another stage direction indicating that Lear also kneels, or tries to kneel, to her. Cordelia's own speech at this point in the scene gives editors the clue to add these stage directions. Her words thus contain implicit stage directions. In the Arden edition these lines read:

CORDELIA [*Kneels.*]   O look upon me, sir,
And hold your hands in benediction o'er me!
[*She restrains him as he tries to kneel.*]
No, sir, you must not kneel.

(4.7.57–9)

These gestures are heartbreaking, especially when we see them in the context of the entire play. On Cordelia's part they show that no matter how cruel her father has been to her, her bond of loyalty to him and her love for him remain unbroken. A child kneeling to a parent is a traditional gesture of respect, and Cordelia kneels as she continues to show deference to her father. But what about Lear? What does it mean that the King kneels or tries to kneel to Cordelia? One possibility is that he is humbling himself as he realizes he has been unworthy of his daughter's continued deference. He may be recognizing that she now has more moral authority than he. The parent has switched places with the child. This is a stupendous reversal from Lear's haughty assumption of infallibility in the play's opening moments.

Other embodied actions in the play are equally ripe for interpretation. Some of these actions have to do with humiliation and even torture: moments when the body is subject to pain and indignities intended to denigrate the person being tormented. One such moment occurs when the disguised Kent, serving as the King's messenger, is put in the stocks before Gloucester's castle after he has spoken rudely to Regan's husband, Cornwall. The stocks were an instrument of punishment in which a person's legs or arms were locked into a wooden device so that the victims were immobilized in a sitting or standing position. Sometimes in marketplaces, those placed in the stocks were pelted with rotten fruit or eggs or stones, and, if their arms were immobilized, they were not even able to wipe away the grime. Sometimes people died in the stocks from the abuse they received.

Ordinarily, nobles were not put in the stocks as it was assumed their high social position exempted them from such lowly forms of punishment. It is, then, a terrible violation of decorum to put the King's messenger in the stocks. Gloucester knows what an insult this is and tries to prevent it. He fails. When Lear arrives at Gloucester's castle, the first thing he says to the immobilized Kent is: 'What's he that hath so much thy place mistook / To set thee here?' (2.2.202–3). The 'place' or social position to which Lear refers is Kent's place as the King's messenger. To humiliate Kent is to disrespect Lear. There is no way an audience can fail to miss this moment of humiliation because Shakespeare keeps Kent onstage in the stocks while nearly 200 lines of dialogue are spoken. He is put in the stocks at line 148 of 2.2 and is not released until line 316. In short, he remains in the stocks, in full view of the audience, for a long time, while other characters enter and exit until his plight becomes a main point of contention between Lear and his daughters and sons-in-law. In a grammar of class-based punishment, the visual image of Kent in the stocks speaks volumes about the king's growing powerlessness and the extremes to which his enemies will go to humiliate him.

Another gesture involving Gloucester serves the same purpose of humiliation. Gloucester attempts to aid the old King and is in communication with Cordelia and her forces. When Cornwall learns this from Edmund, he decides to blind Gloucester as an example of what happens to those whom he considers traitors. The act of blinding Gloucester speaks for itself. It is an act of cruelty and a display of raw physical force that shocks the audience. In performance, playgoers regularly gasp and look aside as one eye, and then another, is gouged out. This moment is preceded, however, by another assault on Gloucester's body that may be less easily legible to those of us who live in the modern era. After Gloucester is tied to a chair, a stage direction reads: [*Regan plucks his beard.*] (s.d. 3.7.34). To which he cries out, 'By the kind gods, 'tis most ignobly done / To pluck me by the beard' (3.7.35–6). The language of this implicit stage direction, which editors use to authorize the stage direction they put in brackets, gives us cues to its social meaning. Gloucester says Regan has acted *ignobly.* The *Oxford English Dictionary* defines the word as meaning *dishonourably, basely.* Gloucester is accusing Regan of acting like a common villain, not a person nobly born. Moreover, in calling on the *kind gods,* he is activating multiple meanings of *kind* including *natural, native, benevolent, of one's own kin.* He implies that the benevolent gods, native to this place, would condemn actions that are unkind, unnatural and not worthy of a kinsman.

As a way of furthering understanding the meaning of Regan's gesture, plucking her host's beard, we should note that beards in the early modern period were a signifier of age. Old men's beards were also a sign of their authority and wisdom. As the above lines imply, to pluck an old man's beard was to humiliate and disrespect the authority granted to such figures, even more so when the old man is an earl, and, as he insists in the following lines, a man acting as the host to Regan and Cornwall. They are not in their own castle, but in his. Hospitality was an important social virtue in the period, and for a guest to humiliate a host, or a host a guest, was a crime against the mutual bonds that were meant to bind society together. Cornwall and Regan, by their actions, are therefore also violating the laws of hospitality, as well as defying the kind gods.

Two final examples will show how powerful the language of embodied gesture can be. These both have to do with Lear in the final third of the play. When Kent has managed to convey him to Dover, the old King slips into madness from grief, humiliation and exposure to the elements. Escaping from his attendants, he roves through the fields near the sea. Cordelia narrates his state as it has been described to her by those who have seen him.

> Alack, 'tis he. Why, he was met even now
> As mad as the vexed sea, singing aloud,
> Crowned with rank fumiter and furrow-weeds,
> With burdocks, hemlock, nettles, cuckoo-flowers,
> Darnel and all the idle weeds that grow
> In our sustaining corn.
>
> (4.4.1–6)

What Cordelia describes are the weeds and flowers with which the old King has fashioned a crown for himself. This becomes an implied stage direction for Lear's actual entry in 4.6.80 when the stage direction reads: *Enter* LEAR *mad [crowned with wild flowers]*. How do we 'read' the language of the flower crown? Well, we might remember the first scene of the play when Lear probably wore a gold or silver crown. It would be an inevitable part of his attire in a formal court setting as long as he retained power and acted the role of the monarch. A flower crown would be an echo of that earlier crown, but so different as to underscore how far Lear has fallen from that opening moment. Fragile flowers and common weeds have replaced a crown of precious metals. The flowers and weeds might suggest something else: perhaps Lear's new connection to the native plants that grow in the soil of Britain. For much of the first two thirds of the play Lear's actions, and his own words, suggest that he has taken too little care of Britain, its people, the well-being of his native soil. He has divided his kingdom, banished his good daughter and best counsellor, and disregarded the suffering of the poor. In a subtle way, the weed and flower crown may suggest that Lear is returning, though in a state of madness, to a connection with the place that he once ruled. Of course, the flower crown also represents Lear's madness. A sane man would not adorn himself in this fashion, but the image of the flower-crowned ex-monarch, suggests that Lear, passing through a purgatory of madness, is now in some genuine relationship to his native land. It is not represented as a place on a map to be divided by an arbitrary line, but a place where real weeds grow and through whose fields and beaches Lear now moves, on foot, alone. Perhaps it is only through such an experience that he can undergo, next, a reconciliation with and recognition of his daughter Cordelia.

That reconciliation is the final moment whose visual grammar I want to parse, focusing on the clothing Lear wears when he is brought onto the stage 'in a chair carried by servants' (s.d. before 4.7.21). In 4.6 we had seen Lear wearing the flower crown. Now he is in 'fresh garments' (4.7.22) that were put on him while he slept. What does this sartorial transformation mean? How does it convey meaning? The answer depends partly on how directors and costume designers clothe the old King. Lear *could* be dressed in royal robes. That would emphasize that Cordelia is attempting to give back to Lear the social position he gave away and that his other two daughters were only too glad to help him lose.

In many productions, however, Lear is dressed in simple white clothes, a choice perhaps emphasizing Lear's purification by suffering or his return to sanity after a period of madness. If unmarked by emblems of his rank, these white clothes might suggest Lear's common humanity, not his monarchical past. The sight of the 'fresh garments', then, does not have a single meaning. Designers can imagine it differently. But some basic contrast between the mad Lear crowned in flowers and the (as we soon find out) sane Lear dressed in fresh garments makes a statement we are invited to interpret. Something like a rebirth is suggested by the visual motif of new clothes. Surrounded by Cordelia, a physician and soft music, the King has come back from a place where he was lost to himself and wildly crowned with flowers and weeds. He at first believes that he has died and that Cordelia is a soul in bliss. It turns out he is on earth but experiencing something like the bliss of heaven in the reunion with that living daughter. You may want to ask, if Lear's clothing signals that he is a new man released from the purgatory of his madness, do his subsequent actions suggest that he has fundamentally changed? What does the text suggest? What do you think and what is your evidence for your point of view?

Writing matters

In this chapter we have been examining the verbal and physical languages through which *King Lear* takes shape as a work of art. Now it is your turn to practise writing about the language of the play focusing on a scene we have not as yet discussed, scene 4 of Act 1. It shows the old King during his first sojourn with his daughter Goneril. Everyone had agreed that Lear and one hundred of his knights would live, by turns, with Goneril and Regan. Almost immediately, however, Goneril begins to back out of this commitment, ordering her servants to treat Lear negligently and treating him less kindly than at first. This scene provides us with the first opportunity to see how Lear will respond to his altered circumstances. At the same time, the scene introduces Kent in his disguise as Caius. We are invited to observe how he behaves in this disguise. Do his actions or his language change? We also are introduced to two crucial new characters, Goneril's servant Oswald and Lear's Fool. What are they like? How do they speak? How would you describe their verbal interactions with Lear?

After carefully reading this scene, please write a response to one or more of the following prompts that will let you practise the kinds of analysis we have been exploring in this chapter. Your answers do not have to be long, but they should be precise (500 words is fine). Focus in on particular words, speeches, brief exchanges or bodily actions, taking note of features that you find interesting and explaining your interpretation of them. In the next chapter we will think more about how to develop an effective argument, but here focus first on careful and patient engagement with the text. What do you notice about Shakespeare's use of language in some pieces of text that you find interesting and important?

1 In this scene are there any keywords that particularly invite you to consider their significance? Are any words repeated often within a speech or across several? Do these words have multiple meanings? Do they mean the same thing to different characters? Words like *fool* or *nothing* might be a place to start your investigation, but there are many others on which you could focus.

2 Take any short speech or part of a speech (ten lines or less) spoken by Goneril or Lear's Fool and write about what you find remarkable about the language of that speech. What unique features does it contain? Is it in prose or verse? Does it use rhyme? Repetition? If it is a poetic passage, is the metre regular? What is the effect of any irregularities it contains? Does it contain puns or other figures of speech? How does the passage contribute to your understanding of the character who is speaking? Does the Goneril of this scene speak differently from the Goneril of scene 1.1? What are some of the unique or remarkable things about the Fool's language?

3 Analyse any short exchange (less than twenty lines) between Kent and Lear or Lear and the Fool. Are there any unique features of the passage you have chosen? Do the speakers echo one another's words? Do they share lines? Do they speak in metrically regular lines? Are any lines particularly short or long or irregular in rhythm? Do the speakers use the same words, but with different meanings? What is the role of questions in the exchange you have chosen? The role of commands? Threats?

4 Look carefully at the stage directions included in your edition of scene 1.4 of *King Lear*. Do any of these stage directions have particular significance? Are the stage directions added by modern editors and placed in brackets effective? Are they necessary? Are there other places where you would add a stage direction? Why? For example, would you give the Fool a real egg to hold at some point in the scene?

5 Are there any significant physical gestures or bodily movements that in your view have special importance in this scene? What are they? How should they be performed? What meanings do they have? As you start to think about this, you

could, for example, look at lines 91–104 in which Lear gives money to Kent for his service and Lear and the Fool then pass a coxcomb (a special hat worn to indicate that someone was a professional fool) back and forth between them. What is the significance of these gestures? How do they convey something that words alone do not capture?

In the next chapter, focusing largely on Act 3 of *Lear*, we will be looking at new aspects of the play's language, namely, the dense web of figurative language that threads through it and also the aural metaphorics of the play's central scenes: the storm on the heath.

CHAPTER TWO

Into the Storm and Out

Metaphor, Symbol, Disguise, Double Plots and Multiple Texts

In this chapter we will focus on important ways to understand the languages through which *King Lear* communicates with audiences and readers, with special attention to metaphor, symbol, disguise and scene juxtapositions. We will build from attending to small linguistic units, like a single metaphor, to compounding images and word clusters that create a cumulative impact over time. Similarly, we will think not only about individual scenes, but about the sequential deployment of several. The overarching goal will be to increase your power to make sense of this harrowing middle section of the tragedy and to expand your ways of analysing its dizzying metaphorical and structural complexity. In this chapter we will therefore focus on some brainstorming exercises that invite you to move from local observations to larger claims. What kinds of questions can you train yourself to ask of a dramatic speech or a dramatic encounter that will allow you to build an argument, not only about those lines or exchanges, but about their importance to the play as a whole? Your toolkit of questions, always based on your developing knowledge of how drama communicates, will let you open up this remarkable play in fresh and interesting ways, ways that matter to you.

Preliminaries

If Acts 1 and 2 of *King Lear* swiftly move the protagonist from the position of all-powerful king to powerless suppliant in the courtyard of Gloucester's castle, the next movement of the play, Acts 3 and 4, turns Lear into a homeless outcast attended by a dwindling band of faithful followers. He is only rescued from this outcast state when Cordelia, returning from France with an army, finds and briefly shelters him. This middle portion of the play is harrowing. Audiences struggle because they are confronted with a seemingly unstoppable cascade of violent and overwhelming events. As we discussed in the prior chapter, few theatregoers can watch the blinding of Gloucester without recoiling in horror, but his blinding is just part of the suffering characters endure and audiences must assimilate as homelessness, mental breakdown, and exposure to rain and cold overtake those outside the castle. Historically, actors have been severely tested as they perform the part of the old King in these scenes, especially if they themselves approach the fictional king's age of 80. Lear has many lines in these acts, and at first he must speak them while contending with the sound effects of a storm and sometimes with the water that accompanies that storm's theatrical simulation.

The emotional impact of this section of the play is peculiarly intensified, moreover, by the sense that many things happen at least twice. For example, the audience not only follows the story of Lear, but also of Gloucester, another old man, one of whose children betrays him. As I suggested in the Introduction to this book, *King Lear* is an unusual tragedy because of this double plot. Both Gloucester and Lear make the wrong choice about which offspring to trust; each endures humiliation and suffering as a result; and each makes his way towards Dover and a long-deferred reconciliation with the child he has spurned. Many critics have explored why the experiences of the two old men are both so similar and yet so different. For Lear, the greatest torments seem to be mental. While he is wet, cold and unprotected on the heath, what he fears most is what eventually comes to pass: madness. To Goneril he says, 'I prithee, daughter, do not make me mad' (2.2.407), and yet he does go mad. His desire for revenge and his long-repressed recognition of his stupendous folly, first brought home to him by the Fool, undo the old King. He is, literally, brainsick, longing for a revenge he cannot achieve, and by turns repentant and defiant, ultimately running through the fields near Dover crowned with flowers and weeds. By contrast, Gloucester's transformation and suffering are, in the first instance, physical in nature, though he, too, suffers remorse and entertains suicidal thoughts. Blinded by Cornwall and Regan, Gloucester stumbles unseeingly towards Dover apparently guided only by a beggarman, Poor Tom. As you work with this section of the play, you may want to ask: why does each man suffer in the particular way he does? How is each defined for us by the way he deals with this suffering? Is one more heroic or insightful than the other? What evidence would you give for your views? Most importantly, we will ask how the stage language of scenic juxtaposition compounds the meaning of each plot. What can we understand of Lear's experience *because* it is implicitly compared to Gloucester's, and vice versa?

It would be a mistake, however, to imagine that the violence enacted and endured in this section of the play is confined to these two old men. Lear's loyal Fool shivers and cries out for shelter. Edgar, disguised as Poor Tom, whom we will discuss further below, suffers from cold, hunger and the loss of the privileged life he has led. Other characters, including Lear, Kent and Gloucester, are appalled by what they take as Poor Tom's wretchedness. Nearly naked, he describes hearing the cries of demons and drinking pond water thick with algae. Early modern audiences would have come to a tragedy with the expectation that their attention would be directed towards a singular figure, the titular character, set apart from other men. In a certain sense *King Lear* follows this pattern. Lear does command much of the audience's attention. Yet with its structures of doubling and repetition, *Lear* creates a countervailing sense that some of the central experiences of the play do not uniquely befall a singular individual but are the common lot of humankind. The middle section of the play is a kind of echo chamber in which the cries of anguish voiced by one character reverberate with the cries of many others. When the rain comes, everyone gets wet; all bodies and all psyches, like all societies, are vulnerable to their own undoing.

The play has often been described as archetypal, that is, telling a story founded on fears shared by many: of bad rulers, cruel parents, deceptive children, humiliation and bodily vulnerability. In such readings, Lear becomes a kind of Everyman and his kingdom an Everyplace. I believe this is at least partly true, though one can certainly also point to the many ways in which the play references events, people and concerns peculiar to the early seventeenth century when it was written. Like James I, who ruled England when Shakespeare wrote the play, Lear imagines himself as a monarch with absolute powers, an illusion quickly shattered. Similarly, fools had an established social role in European courts in this period, as does Lear's Fool; and Poor Tom speaks to the psychic and economic precarity of the Jacobean underclass. Yet if Lear is of its time, it also anticipates the many future moments in which people have felt devastating precarity, no more so than in the twentieth and twenty-first centuries when the play has been staged in the context of World Wars, the threat of atomic annihilation, catastrophic global warming, and the mass migration of untold numbers of people displaced from their homes with no one willing to receive them. *King Lear* speaks to one historical moment and to many, records the suffering of singular people and of multitudes. Nowhere do we feel that more strongly than in the maelstrom of Act 3 and the carnage it leaves in its wake in Act 4.

Metaphors

In the previous chapter we spoke of *King Lear*'s heightened language. We explored some of the principles of repetition, balance and contrast that structure Shakespeare's dramatic language, and we analysed how devices like onomatopoeia and isocolon are used to make the play more effective, whether read or performed. One of the most basic kinds of figurative language found everywhere in Shakespeare is metaphor. Metaphor is a device by which something (the tenor of the metaphor) is explained by or compared to a different thing (the vehicle of the metaphor). The two things are not identical but share some qualities or properties that are revealed by the comparison. For example, if I say: 'Delores is a tiger,' I don't literally mean that Delores, the girl, is a wild animal belonging to the cat family. Rather, I probably mean that some of the qualities of a tiger (its power, its energy, maybe its reputation for ferocity) help to explain Delores's nature or actions. Had I said: 'Delores is like a tiger,' I would be making more explicit that a comparison is being made between Delores and the tiger. A comparison made in this way is called a simile, signalled by the use of *like* or *as* to join the two things being compared. A metaphor is less explicit about the terms of the comparison, inviting the reader's full participation in realizing the potentially wide range of meanings released by the friction between tenor and vehicle.

Metaphoric language is one of the most important ways that the rich suggestiveness, and sometimes the mystery, of Shakespeare's language is enhanced. It is also a way in which meaning is multiplied, since a metaphor or simile makes us consider at least two things at once – in our very simple comparison, Delores and a tiger – and invites us to make a cognitive or affective connection between them. The result is a new concept: the tiger-like qualities of Delores. Often the reader has to work to bring the two aspects of a metaphor together or even to make the terms of the comparison legible. For example, there is a searing moment when Regan and Cornwall have discovered through Edmund that Gloucester is aiding the old King. Gloucester has been bound to a chair and his beard cruelly plucked by Regan. As Cornwall and Regan question him, they keep asking why Lear has gone to Dover. Finally, Gloucester realizes he cannot escape answering. This exchange follows:

GLOUCESTER
  I am tied to the stake and I must stand the course.
REGAN Wherefore to Dover, sir?
GLOUCESTER
  Because I would not see thy cruel nails
  Pluck out his poor old eyes; nor thy fierce sister
  In his anointed flesh stick boarish fangs.

(3.7.53–7)

There are two elements of this exchange I want to examine. The first is Gloucester's initial line: 'I am tied to the stake and I must stand the course.' Here the terms of the metaphor are implied rather than stated directly and depend on the audience's knowledge of a popular early modern blood sport: bear-baiting. When a bear was baited or provoked, it was usually chained to a stake in the middle of an arena and then dogs were set loose to attack it. Often the dogs were injured or killed by a swipe of the bear's paw; sometimes the bear's flesh was ripped apart by the teeth of the dogs. Either party in this encounter could end up dead or dying.

When Gloucester says he is tied to a stake and must stand the course (meaning the time that the contest between bear and the dogs would last), he implicitly compares his chair to the bear-baiting stake, himself to a bear, and Cornwall and Regan to dogs. These comparisons have many implications. First, Gloucester's speech expresses his sense of being degraded and powerless – neither he nor the bear can unbind their fetters – and vulnerable to torture. The premise of bear-baiting is the death or wounding of the animals made to fight with one another before a crowd of bloodthirsty spectators. Gloucester sees himself as such a tormented animal. But the metaphor also expresses the inhuman nature of his antagonists. They are like the dogs lacerating the chained bear and, by extension, Gloucester's own flesh. Regan and Cornwall, however, have *chosen* to become like vicious dogs, binding their aged host, threatening and then mutilating him. Gloucester, by contrast, has not chosen his helpless situation but has had it forced upon him. Trying to maintain decorum in his castle and to follow the laws of hospitality, he has just returned from attempting to get the old King to shelter after vainly imploring Regan and Cornwall to themselves offer Lear such aid. Through the implicit metaphor of the bear chained to the stake, then, Gloucester has cast himself as the injured party consigned to his fate by humans dog-like in their viciousness. Rather than a place of hospitality and shelter, his castle has become, his metaphorical language suggests, a common bear-baiting arena, soiled by blood and debased by unworthy acts.

An irony of this scene, moreover, is that what Gloucester fears will happen to Lear's body – that his eyes will be gouged out and his flesh wounded – is exactly what happens to Gloucester himself. Soon after the speech we have been examining, Regan and Cornwall blind Gloucester, a stage event terrible in itself, but one that may also recall for many audience members the torment of the famous blind bear, Harry Hunks. The whipping of this bear was described by commentators who saw bear-baiting at an arena south of the River Thames where the Globe Theatre, at which *King Lear* was performed, was located. The metaphorical resonances of Gloucester's bear-baiting metaphor could well have extended to this local animal 'celebrity'. Mutilated and bleeding and then thrust out of doors to 'smell' his way to Dover, the old Earl may have seemed to some theatregoers all too like the blind bear whose torment they had witnessed and, perhaps, had cheered on. Human savagery, certainly as great as the savagery of any animal, and often directed against the animal world as well as against other humans, is on full display at such moments, confounding, as we will see, any claim to human moral superiority.

The second metaphor I want to underscore seems in some ways to grow from the first and involves Gloucester's characterization of what he would spare the old King. He would spare him the horror of having his middle daughter pluck out his eyes with her nails and his older daughter from sinking 'boarish fangs' into his flesh. If Gloucester sees himself as a chained bear attacked by dogs, he here imagines Lear attacked by a daughter's 'nails' and then by another animal, a boar. Again, at the risk of saying the obvious, Goneril is not a boar, a wild animal with tusks that could gore a person's flesh. But she is boar-like in her savagery, a savagery shown by stripping Lear of his knights and colluding with his exclusion from Gloucester's castle. Here Gloucester's language suggests that Goneril would go even further and physically attack her father. The horror of this imagined assault is compounded by the fact that, in the early modern period, a king had an almost god-like status. At his coronation, his flesh was anointed with holy oil. There is not only cruelty, but also sacrilege, in what Gloucester implies these daughters will do if they rend and pierce the body of an anointed king. Unable, however, at this moment to wound Lear directly, Regan and Cornwall momentarily turn their fury on their host.

It is worth pausing, however, to consider further the relationship between the terms of these human–animal comparisons. If cruel people are compared to animals, does that mean that animals are inherently inferior to humans, or at least lacking in the morals, the tender-heartedness or the bravery that, in some quarters, are assumed to make humans superior to these 'brute beasts'? There is no simple answer to this question. Many times in *Lear* animal comparisons are used negatively, to critique humans who fail to act in a way worthy of their supposedly superior nature. These comparisons often impute to animals qualities of viciousness or cruelty that humans themselves display. Sometimes, however, animal–human comparisons directly or subtly highlight the ways in which animals are revealed to be superior to humans. When Gloucester compares himself to a bear chained to a stake, this is also the moment when he first openly begins to resist Regan and Cornwall, rather than doing it secretly. In comparing himself to a chained bear, Gloucester not only calls attention to his enforced suffering, but also displays some of the qualities associated with bears in the early modern period, including dignity and courage. The bear can model how humans might endure torment imposed on them by other humans. As you engage with the middle sections of the play, consider how, at different moments, the relative value or worth of animals and humans is depicted, and the many ways humans project human qualities onto the animal world, often ignoring the autonomy of those creatures or their unique forms of intelligence and sociality. In thinking about the lines we have been investigating, we might remember that it is humans who train dogs to bait bears, just as it is humans who have decided that dogs are appropriate metaphors for humans who behave cruelly. Possessing the power of human speech, men and women largely impose *their* meanings on the animal world.

As I have suggested, however, at least some human–animal comparisons in *King Lear* challenge the idea of human exceptionalism. By this I mean the idea that humankind has unusual qualities that make people superior to other creatures and justified in their dominance of them. We might consider another moment at the beginning of Act 3 to see how this challenge can be underscored. When 3.1 begins, Kent is describing to a knight how madly Lear is behaving, fruitlessly commanding the storm to do his bidding and exposing himself to wind and rain. Kent says:

> This night wherein the cub-drawn bear would couch,
> The lion and the belly-pinched wolf
> Keep their fur dry, unbonneted he runs,
> And bids what will take all.
>
> (3.1.12–15)

Kent contrasts Lear's behaviour to that of three animals: a bear, a lion and a wolf. The bear, having nursed its cub, is undoubtedly hungry. The wolf is described as 'belly-pinched' (13). We think of a lion as always on the prowl for prey. Yet these three hungry creatures all sense that this is a night when they should stay under cover. The bear 'couches' (12) or goes into its den; the lion and wolf 'keep their fur dry' (14), presumably by seeking shelter. Only Lear, 'unbonneted' (14), that is, with his head uncovered, recklessly runs into the storm and 'bids what will take all' (15). This last phrase means something like 'let the devil take all' or 'let ruin come'. The implicit comparison between the behaviour of the beasts and the king does not show Lear to advantage. Unlike bear, lion or wolf, he does not have the wit to preserve himself from the storm. Instead, it takes all the effort of Kent and the Fool to bring him to the wretched hovel where they hope to shelter him from the storm's ravages. The passage reverses the hierarchy that places humans above the other beasts; members of the animal world here seem more instinctively intelligent than the King himself. It is a continuing question whether the humans in *King Lear* are distinguished more by their grandeur or by their vulnerability and limitations, and whether their pretensions to dominion over other creatures are justified.

Symbols

There is much more one can say about how and why metaphors involving animals permeate the middle movement of *King Lear*. You may want to jot down other examples of human–animal comparisons that you find significant. You can also, of course, identify other chains or clusters of metaphors that do not draw on the animal world. I want now, however, to turn to another form of figurative language found in this part of the play, namely the presence of *symbols*. In literary contexts, a symbol is understood as a word, object or situation that represents something else, often an abstract concept. Like the metaphors we have so far discussed, a symbol suggests language's potential for multiplying meaning. A symbol often has a concrete or physical referent but implies a host of other meanings. For example, if a rich man in a short story is repeatedly shown polishing his fancy, expensive car and parking it in the driveway for everyone to see, we might say that for him the car is a symbol of his wealth and his pride in that wealth. In Act 3 of *King Lear* one potential symbol dominates all others: the storm that permeates the act from first to last. We are reminded of the storm's presence over and over; it is created and highlighted both by verbal references and by stage effects that accumulate over time.

These effects become part of the general soundscape of the performance. The storm is first heard at the end of Act 2. As Lear proclaims that 'I'll not weep' (2.2.472), the Folio stage direction reads: '*Storm and Tempest.*' Almost immediately Cornwall and the daughters begin discussing this storm and their decision to shut the castle against Lear's party. A few lines later, Act 3 opens with the Folio stage direction: '*Storm still.*' Thereafter, as talk of the storm continues, it is also a staged reality that announces its own ongoing presence. Directors differ on how much rain, wind, thunder and lightning they want to create in the theatre, but the stage directions indicate that the storm must have some material embodiment.

This natural phenomenon is so terrifying and so pervasively present in performance that it invites a symbolic reading. What is the storm's larger meaning? Of what is it a symbol? This is an important and hotly debated question. As always, we should look to the play's text for answers, realizing that there may well be multiple possibilities. One place to start is the immediate context surrounding specific stage directions indicating that the storm is heard or seen. For example, just before the stage direction '*Storm and Tempest.*' at 2.2.472, Lear has said: 'You think I'll weep, / No, I'll not weep' (2.2.471–2). As he struggles to avoid his tears from flowing, the storm begins to rage. This juxtaposition suggests an implicit comparison between Lear's grief, fury and frustration, and the intensity of the storm. The storm raging *around* the old King is like the emotional maelstrom raging *within* him. The storm thus can be read as a symbol of Lear's internal anguish, storm-like in its intensity. It symbolizes his suffering. This reading, of course, spotlights Lear as a tragic protagonist whose inner turmoil is simply amplified through the storm-like stage effects created around him. It may also suggest that Lear is a victim against whom outrages have been committed, outrages that have produced the inner storm within the old King.

But how else might we approach the question of the storm as symbol? Are there any passages in which Lear directly addresses the storm? If so, that might tell us how *he* gives it a more-than-literal meaning. Turn to the beginning of 3.2, when the old King directly addresses the storm in a way that gradually reveals a startling and not altogether unexpected dimension of his interpretive relationship to this natural happening. Lear addresses the storm as if it were an extension of his own power, a servant to his will. He says:

Blow winds and crack your cheeks! Rage, blow!
You cataracts and hurricanoes, spout
Till you have drenched our steeples, drowned the cocks!
You sulphurous and thought-executing fires,
Vaunt-couriers of oak-cleaving thunderbolts,
Singe my white head! And thou, all-shaking thunder,
Strike flat the thick rotundity o'the world,
Crack nature's mould, all germens spill at once
That make ungrateful man!

(3.2.1–9)

In Chapter 1 we noted the prominence of imperative verbs in these lines. Whatever else Lear may think about the storm, he regards its elements (water, lightning and thunder [cataracts, fires, thunderbolts]) as his to command. They are told to blow, rage, drench, singe, strike and crack, amplifying and extending the powers he imagines he has. Because Jupiter as a pagan god was often depicted with a thunderbolt as a sign of his power, Lear seems to be commanding this deity, as well, when he orders the 'all-shaking thunder' (l. 6) to do his bidding. For Lear, the storm becomes a symbol of his own imagined powers, gargantuan in their ambition, and an indication that his will can be imposed both on nature and the gods.

What Lear commands, furthermore, the 'all-shaking thunder' to *do* opens a complex metaphorical sequence that is both disturbing and revelatory. Lear orders the thunder god to flatten the rounded parts of the earth and to break open the container (the 'mould') that holds the seeds (the 'germens') that allow the earth to be fertile and flourish. These lines implicitly compare the fertile earth struck by lightning to a female womb, rounded in pregnancy, holding male semen, but broken open by an external force. Lear's command, horrible in its wish to destroy the forces that together create life, is also misogynist in the violence it imagines visiting upon the feminized body of the earth. This violent fantasy undoubtedly springs from Lear's hatred of the actions of his two elder daughters. In willing the storm to enact his vengeance, moreover, Lear assumes no blame for what has befallen him. His focus is entirely on punishing those whom he believes have wronged him and caused his present pain.

Shakespearean figurative language is frequently elliptical, multivalent and cascading. One metaphor builds fast upon another in moments of heightened emotion, and the terms of an implicit metaphor are often signalled by a single word or phrase such as *stake* or *nature's mould*. In the case of the storm, the multiplicity of implications created by it forbid a single reading of its symbolic possibilities. The storm, we have recognized, may partly function as a symbol of the old King's internal grief and suffering. Looking carefully at how Lear addresses the storm and noting how Lear instrumentalizes this natural phenomenon, treating it if were just one of the many people or forces he attempts to control by his will, we could say the storm is for him symbolic of the titanic power he would exert over his chosen enemies.

If we step back from Lear's perspective, however, and remember his initial irrational behaviour and his cruelty to Cordelia and Kent, we might also see a third option, not available to Lear himself: perhaps the storm is symbolic of the wrath of the gods, punishing Lear for his folly. Rather than being in command of the winds, the rain and the thunder god, perhaps Lear is being scourged and punished by them for his pretension and his folly. After all, whatever Lear thinks about his power to command, he and Gloucester are the ones suffering; their enemies are safely tucked inside Gloucester's castle. When you consider the possible symbolic meanings of the storm, what argument would you choose to make about it, and how would you justify your answer?

Human beings constantly impose meaning on events around them. In our daily lives we often create symbolic readings of people, things and situations. The storm in *Lear* is such a big and omnipresent event in the middle of the play that it invites us to read it as more than just a natural occurrence. But what if it is a mistake to make the storm a symbol? Maybe it is simply a storm, and we should read no further meaning into it. Rather than in anyone's command, human or divine, the storm may simply be a powerful natural phenomenon that can create misery for the humans caught in its fury. From one perspective this may be perhaps its most frightening implication: the storm may have no other meaning than as a manifestation of nature's power, which is insensible to humanity's needs or prayers. This can seem like a bleak prospect. What if there are no gods to observe our suffering, judge our enemies or address our needs?

The play, we might remember, is set in pre-Christian times. References to 'the gods' in the play – and you may want to seek these out and analyse their meaning – are therefore to pagan deities. We have seen how the Roman 'thunder god', Jupiter, was obliquely referenced by Lear in the opening speech of 3.2. But critics have long debated whether any divine power is present in the world of *Lear*. As you read the play, do you see the gods at work in it? What evidence would you give for your point of view? Are the gods in some way behind the storm Lear experiences? If so, whose side are they on? Many thorny questions arise from the ambiguities surrounding the question of supernatural forces at work in the play. Does the human desire for 'justice' or for the presence of gods mean that gods or justice exist? If the gods do not exist, or if they remain unknowable or indifferent to humankind, how does one ground an ethical life and promote justice without a religious code to establish norms of behaviour? Rather than call on the gods to punish imagined enemies, what else could Lear do to ameliorate the suffering for which he is at least partly responsible? This is an important question for all readers of the play.

To complicate further the issue of how the storm functions in *Lear* and how humans might live morally should there be no gods or at least no gods who care about them, I want to direct attention to a moment when Lear himself seems to take on board these questions. When he does so, he stops addressing the storm directly and for a moment seems to regard it as a natural phenomenon whose effects on ordinary people should be his chief concern. This moment occurs when Lear is led by the Fool and Gloucester to the hovel where Poor Tom has taken shelter. Lear suddenly seems, in the middle of the pelting storm, to recognize the suffering of another human being, someone right in front of him: his Fool. Notice how Lear's speech changes from the harsh imperatives and howls of rage he has been producing. Instead, Lear kindly urges the Fool to seek shelter in the hovel while Lear himself pauses to pray. In a gesture whose significance we have previously explored, Lear 'kneels' (s.d. 3.4.28), and then he says some of the most beautiful lines in the play:

> Poor naked wretches, wheresoe'er you are,
> That bide the pelting of this pitiless storm,
> How shall your houseless heads and unfed sides,
> Your looped and windowed raggedness, defend you
> From seasons such as these? O, I have ta'en

     Too little care of this. Take physic, pomp,
     Expose thyself to feel what wretches feel,
     That thou mayst shake the superflux to them
     And show the heavens more just.

(3.4.28–36)

Dwelling on the specific bodily details of people whose heads are not protected by a house, whose torsos (sides) are unfed, and whose ragged clothing is full of holes that appear like windows in their garments, Lear wonders how they will endure the merciless storm. The speech is affecting partly in its simplicity. It uses alliteration, the repetition of the 'p' sound in *pelting* and *pitiless*, to suggest the violence of the rain beating down, and it makes naked wretches nothing more than the sum of their body parts and torn clothes.

     Lear here sees the storm, not as something affecting only him or that he can control, but something that everyone experiences, and the poor more terribly than anyone else. At least for this moment, Lear relinquishes his preoccupation with his own victimhood and sees himself as a privileged man who should have taken care of his subjects, especially the poor wretches he has just described. The imperatives in his speech, you may note, become directed at himself, not at the heavens or the storm: 'Take physic, pomp' (33), that is, cure yourself, proud man, and, in sharing in the bodily suffering of the poor, learn to give them the 'superflux' (35) or surplus of your great wealth. If he does, Lear will 'show the heavens more just' (36). This is an odd and moving formulation in that it suggests that it is *man*'s good actions that make people believe in a just heaven. One cannot wait for the gods, if they exist, to act; men must create the just world for which they wish. Then others will believe there is justice in heaven because it is achieved on earth. This moment feels like a moral advance; it seems as if Lear has learned to feel with his fellow man through a shared bodily vulnerability; and that from this recognition he has begun to understand the obligations that he has, as king, to care for and think about his ordinary subjects and not just himself.

     The astonishingly tragic thing about this moment, however, is how quickly it passes. Lear walks no straightforward path from folly to enlightenment, which is the comforting story that people often tell about tragedy as a genre. Sometimes it is we the readers and audience who make the important journeys of discovery as we experience an early modern tragedy. The protagonist's journey is often tortured, unclear and contradictory. As you read through to the end of the play, ask yourself whether you believe Lear changes and, if so, in what way. Can we say he grows and learns, though 80 years old? Or do his best insights, as here, fall away under the pressure of his sorrow, age and self-involvement? Just after Lear has knelt in prayer, his Fool in terror rushes from the hovel followed by Edgar disguised as Poor Tom, and the shock unhinges Lear's sanity. Immediately he reverts to his old habit of seeing the world through the lens of his own suffering. Beholding Poor Tom's wretched state, Lear's first words are: 'Didst thou give all to thy two daughters? And art thou come to this?' (3.4.48–9). Lear can only make sense of Tom's predicament as a mirror of his own. Lear's moral awakening seems at best to have been transitory, not a lasting example of man's exceptional capacity for growth and insight. As Lear engages further with Poor Tom, however, many of the issues we have been discussing are given vivid, concrete and complicated expression in the person of the Bedlam beggar.

Poor Tom and the language of disguise

As always in drama, it is not only verbal language that is important but also how the play uses other languages of performance. We have been talking about how metaphoric and symbolic language multiplies meaning, opening up possibilities for multifaceted comparisons between one thing and another: a man and a bear, a storm and all the things the storm might symbolize. In the middle sections of the play, other ways of doubling and multiplying the significance of the action are utilized. To begin to explore these strategies, I want to focus first on Poor Tom/Edgar. As we begin to explore this riveting figure, and the many functions he performs in the play, write down details about his actions and appearance in Act 3. Be as concrete as you can because you are creating an archive of textual details that you can eventually use to brainstorm ideas about Poor Tom's significance in the play and his connection to other figures and themes in it. How, for example, is Tom dressed? How does he talk? How do others interact with or treat him? Remember, of course, that Poor Tom is 'really' Edgar, the legitimate son of Gloucester. In Act 2, we watched him assume the disguise of

Poor Tom to escape from the men who were hunting him. If you go back to the speech in which he describes his transformation, you may find clues as to how he will look and act as the Bedlam beggar, a creature 'brought near to beast' (2.2.180). There Edgar says:

> My face I'll grime with filth,
> Blanket my loins, elf all my hair in knots
> And with presented nakedness outface
> The winds and persecutions of the sky.
> The country gives me proof and precedent
> Of Bedlam beggars, who, with roaring voices,
> Strike in their numbed and mortified bare arms
> Pins, wooden pricks, nails, sprigs of rosemary;

> (2.2.180–7)

Notice the specificity of this description. Edgar rubs dirt in his face, clothes himself with only a blanket around his private parts, twists his hair in knots, speaks with a roaring voice, and mutilates himself by sticking sharp objects in his skin: pins, wooden slivers, nails, rosemary. It is no wonder Lear's fool is terrified and thinks a fiend from hell has been hiding in the hovel.

Tom's 'otherness', his fearful appearance and wild and whirring language – a mixture of songs, nonsense words, self-accusations and lamentations – is, of course, a deliberate strategy that Edgar adopts to prevent him from being taken for what he was but a short time ago: a nobleman like Kent and others with whom he shares the stage. The audience's memory of what Edgar was, and its apprehension of what he has made himself, graphically underscore his precarity and vulnerability. Anyone, from bad luck, poverty or illness, can come to Poor Tom's state.

The power of the moment depends on Shakespeare's skilful use of one of the oldest of theatrical devices: disguise. In one sense, disguise lies at the root of all theatre. Actors play parts. Onstage, they are not themselves, but someone else, and their transformation often depends on assuming clothes that signify the separateness of characters from the actors impersonating them. In the case of Edgar/ Poor Tom, the form of disguise common to all acting practice is doubled. A character, here Edgar, pretends for an extended period of time to be someone else, Poor Tom. The audience, having seen Edgar put on his Poor Tom disguise in 2.2, cannot ever entirely forget the Edgar figure who morphed before its eyes into a beggarman. Sometimes, Poor Tom speaks in asides during Act 3, and at such moments he is once more Edgar, addressing himself directly to the audience so that the spectators can never forget the 'reality' under his terrifying disguise. You might want to seek out some of those moments and jot down ideas about the effect of having Edgar occasionally 'break out' of his assumed character to reveal his true identity. What is the effect of such moments, and how do they change the nature of the audience's theatrical experience?

Because of an audience's awareness of the superimposed figures of Edgar and Poor Tom, spectators witness two kinds of suffering: the suffering and shame of Edgar who has lost his property, his place in his father's house and his bodily form; and the dreadful physical and mental suffering of Poor Tom, the persona he has adopted. Moreover, Poor Tom is himself a representative figure for a whole group of early modern people, Bedlam beggars. This was the name given to people who had once been housed in Bethlehem Hospital (*Bedlam* is a shortened form of *Bethlehem*), a prison-like institution for the insane established in London in the fifteenth century and in operation when Shakespeare wrote *King Lear*. When released, these mad folk often travelled the countryside begging. Poor Tom is a figure for their collective suffering. He is himself, and all of them, even as he is also a nobleman, Edgar, brought low by treachery and finding in Poor Tom the most apt representation of his outcast state. Poor Tom, then, is one of the most complicated of all the figures Shakespeare created for this play, a theatrical concatenation of various forms of bodily suffering and social humiliation. Disguise is the stage language for making these meanings legible. At the end of this chapter, you will be invited to consider a further step in the gradual process by which Edgar slowly disentangles himself from his disguise and partially recaptures his lost social position.

The audience, however, is not the only entity affected by the distressing appearance of Poor Tom. King Lear has his own response to what he takes to be the figure of a madman bursting out of the hovel in the middle of Act 3, right after Lear has knelt in prayer. To understand the effect that Tom has on Lear, start with a slow reading of 3.4.45–107. Here Edgar as Poor Tom narrates his intense suffering and offers a jumbled biography of his life, claiming that once he was a serving man of dissolute habits. Lear, curious, presses

Tom to answer his questions, interrogating the madman, even while insisting that Tom must have had evil daughters who are to blame for his suffering. Pick out some word clusters, metaphors or repetitions in these lines that illuminate how Tom presents himself and how Lear responds. For example, Poor Tom enters to Lear from the hovel with the line: 'Away, the foul fiend follows me' (3.4.45). If you read what follows, you will see that the language of fiends and foul fiends is repeated often in ensuing speeches. Many people in the early modern period believed that demonic possession could account for mad behaviour. Edgar, the mastermind behind this disguise, is pretending that his Poor Tom is a person tormented and possessed by devils. That would explain some of the fantastical language Tom employs. These references might also suggest that for Edgar's Poor Tom, life on earth, where he is forced to eat toads and shiver naked in a storm, is like a demon-ridden hell. Recently, critics have argued that the begrimed face of Edgar/Poor Tom and his talk of demons link him both to the blackness associated in Christian thought with the devil and also to the Africans beginning to be seen in Jacobean London in increasing numbers as a result of England's quickening involvement with the slave-owning countries of the Iberian peninsula and the importation of Black 'servants' to London. Poor Tom is thus also a racialized figure, his abjection stemming from several intertwined social factors. Edgar's disguise is part of the performance language through which these multiple meanings are embodied.

To a character like the Fool, Poor Tom is simply frightening; others, like Gloucester, look at him with pity, almost at times seeming to recognize the lost son, Edgar, beneath the disguise. But Lear's response is the most startling, partly because he fixates on Tom's near nakedness, and not entirely with horror. Public adult nakedness is striking, of course; from the time human babies are born, in most cultures they are quickly clothed. As infants they are wrapped in swaddling blankets or slung in tight-fitting baby carriers on the backs or chests of caregivers. Even in hot climates, most people wear clothing if only to cover their genital area; wearing clothes is typically taken as one of the things distinctive to human beings. Tom, however, wears almost no clothing, and Lear responds first with pity and then something akin to admiration. He says:

Why, thou wert better in a grave than to answer with thy uncovered body this extremity of the skies. Is man no more than

this? Consider him well. Thou ow'st the worm no silk, the beast
no hide, the sheep no wool, the cat no perfume. Ha? Here's three
on's us are sophisticated; thou art the thing itself. Unaccommodated
man is no more but such a poor, bare forked animal as thou art.
Off, off, you lendings: come, unbutton here.
                [*Tearing at his clothes, he is restrained by Kent and his Fool.*]
                                    Enter GLOUCESTER, *with a torch.*
                                                        (3.4.99–107)

As you consider Lear's drive to remove his own clothing, remember
how Lear must have been dressed as the play opened and he
appeared at the centre of his court world. Why does a man who
once possessed every kind of sartorial adornment, seeing Tom's
nakedness, try to replicate it by ripping off his own clothes?

Consider, too, how this passage fits into the play's repeated
return to lists of beasts. Here, Lear lists three animals who are used
to supply people with clothing. Silk is taken from silkworms, leather
from cattle, wool from sheep. In each case, animals are utilized to
serve human needs, supplying people with clothing, often at the
cost of their own lives. Leather, for example, only comes from dead
cattle. The cat, however, produces a luxury item, perfume, not
something people need to survive, but something they need to feed
their vanity. In each instance, animals are subordinated to human
need or desire. When Lear sees Tom without clothing he suddenly
seems to see, however, not human superiority, but a truth about
human vulnerability. 'Unaccommodated', without the clothing that
is the 'lendings' of the beasts, Tom is but another 'poor, bare, forked
animal', more helpless than most beasts because of his inability to
weather the elements without the coverings taken from other
creatures.

This is a great textual moment on which to exercise your
interpretive skills. Do some brainstorming, focusing on the language
of the scene and its relationship to the surrounding action. How is
Lear reseeing humans' relationship to the animal world? Why does
he call Tom a 'forked animal'? What truth about his own condition
does the nakedness of Poor Tom drive home? Is this moment
primarily showing that Lear has gone mad as he struggles to free
himself from his clothing, or does insight emerge amid his apparent
madness? Does Lear for the first time see that he is in some profound
way *kin* to people in the lowest social orders and perhaps to the

animal world as well? Is the king implying that the essence of man is found in something other than the marks of privilege and power invested in clothes, crowns and sweet-smelling perfumes? Take a few moments and write about this encounter between king and fake madman, choosing one element of it that seems to you particularly important, such as the language of Tom or of Lear, the visual elements of the scene, the import of the stage directions.

Remember that stage directions added by modern editors are placed in brackets. In this case, in the Arden edition of the text a stage direction, '[*Tearing at his clothes, he is restrained by Kent and the Fool*]', was not in either of the original texts of the play. Do you think this stage direction is warranted or useful? What Lear himself has said is that he wants to pull off his 'lendings', that is, his clothes, and asks someone to undo his buttons. Is it more effective to have him restrained from ripping off his clothes or to have him achieve nakedness? Some actors have, indeed, taken off all their clothes for at least part of this scene. Which choice would you advocate and why? Be sure to use your text to show how your choice emerges from textual elements that, for example, have foregrounded clothing earlier in the play or that have concerned themselves with nakedness, with unclothed animals, or with Lear's disregard or recognition of the condition of others. At this point, all the notes you have taken highlighting specific aspects of the presentation of Poor Tom and his first encounter with Lear become the raw material you can now shape into your own argument about some aspect of this crucial encounter. Dramatic meaning in part arises from the gradual unfolding of ideas built up from repeated images, word clusters and visual motifs. Consider, then, how this moment builds on and complicates what has preceded it. You might note, too, that this initial conversation between Lear and Poor Tom concludes when Gloucester arrives, carrying a torch, a ray of kindly light emerging from hellish darkness. Does it signal a turn for the better in the fortunes of Lear, or not?

Doubles: castle and heath, the two texts

As I have been suggesting throughout this book, plays are composed of words but speak to us in other ways as well. As we have just seen, they employ the physical language of disguise and of gestures, such as kneeling, and the non-verbal sounds of trumpets blaring or a storm raging. All these elements, whether we hear and see them during production or only imagine them in silent reading, contribute to what the play 'means' and how it makes us 'feel'. Plays also communicate through the arrangement of scenes, and that arrangement is quite striking in the middle portion of *King Lear*. In early modern theatre, the scene was the most fundamental building block. Scenes ended when the stage was completely cleared of actors before a new group appeared to commence the next scene. Early modern texts sometimes marked scenes in the printed versions while paying no attention to act divisions. In the theatre, a sheet of paper listing the order of the play's scenes was hung up backstage so that actors would know when they needed to be ready to go onstage. This sheet, called a *plat,* also listed the props each scene required so that actors could carry them onstage as needed.

Shakespeare was a master at scenic arrangement. As we discussed in the Introduction to this book, in *King Lear* we can discern a pattern of large, public group scenes through which an audience can chart the King's changing position vis-à-vis those over whom he exerts, or once exerted, monarchical power. These scenes form a kind of spine visually marking Lear's progression from angry tyrant at the very centre of public power to his exclusion from that position of power before Gloucester's castle to his final indifference to the public realm and the demands of rule at the moment of Cordelia's death. But there are many other ways in which Shakespeare orchestrates a meaningful dramatic experience by juxtaposing big group scenes with intimate ones, scenes written entirely in prose with those in verse, and so forth. In the middle movement of *King Lear*, the doubled action of the two plots (the Lear story and the Gloucester story) is structured and made meaningful by sustained juxtaposition of scenes from these two storylines.

In order to analyse this language of scenic juxtaposition by which the two plots are simultaneously advanced while also implicitly commented upon by one another, let's begin by making a scene chart. Go through Act 3 and briefly jot down where each scene seems to occur, who is present in it, and what actions it involves. You will quickly note that the location of a scene frequently has to be discerned from language within the scene, though some editors add brief indications of location at the top of a scene or in the footnotes at the bottom of the page. For example, the stage direction before the opening lines of 3.1 gives us some important information: '*Storm still. Enter* KENT [*disguised*] *and a* Knight *severally.*' From this direction and the lines of dialogue that follow, we know that the scene occurs outside during a storm where the disguised Kent and a new character, a nameless Knight, discuss the old King's desperate situation and Kent imparts information about forces friendly to the King coming to Dover. Kent orders the Knight to go there, bearing a ring as token of Kent's identity, to inform Cordelia of her sisters' unkind treatment of their father. This scene is a prelude to what follows. It ushers in a night of storm; it prepares the audience to see the King and his Fool contending, all alone, with the fierceness of the weather; and allows the audience to hope that help in the person of Cordelia may be coming. As it turns out, that help does not reach Lear for two long acts, and then the army of Cordelia is defeated. Hope never flourishes long in this play, but at the beginning of Act 3 the audience does not yet fully know how true that is.

Take up the trail yourself now by preparing a chart of the remaining scenes in this act. Make a list of significant variables from scene to scene, thinking about what effects are created as the audience moves from a scene involving Lear to one involving Gloucester or his son Edmund. When you make your scene chart, possible factors to note might include scenes inside/scenes outside; many people/few people; bodies richly dressed/bodies ill-clothed or naked; prose/verse; clear speech/mad, riddling, opaque speech; sound effects/no sound effects; physical violence/psychic violence; darkness/light. Once you have your archive of evidence gathered from a careful reading of the entire act, begin to draw conclusions and make arguments from that evidence. For example, do we have expectations about what it is like to be outside during a storm, rather than inside, that are complicated or queried by this sequence of scenes? Is being in the castle a better place to be? For whom? Why does Shakespeare withhold the worst physical violence of this sequence, the blinding of Gloucester, until the seventh scene of this act? What is the effect of its occurring in the castle, a place of supposed shelter? How is the impact of this scene enhanced or affected by its coming as the last action in this series of scenes? Would you say that the sequencing of scenes invites an audience to see similarities between the two old men, Lear and Gloucester, or does the sequencing accentuate differences? What about the 'minor characters' in these scenes? Does the sequencing reveal something about who mitigates suffering and who increases it? Does this correlate with those in certain kinds of clothing or holding certain social positions? We have discussed how learning to read a play depends on paying careful attention to verbal language: words, lines, blocks of dialogue; to metaphoric language and to word clusters threading in suggestive ways through the body of a text. It also depends on reading the language of stagecraft: props, costume, sound and light, noise and silence, massed bodies and single bodies as these follow one another across the temporal unfolding of a performance or imagined performance. The middle section of *King Lear* is a wonderful place to exercise your critical creativity in noting the language of Shakespeare's stagecraft and deciding how it helps to construct some of the deepest meanings of the play.

However, I now want to complicate the exercise I just encouraged you to undertake. Many things seem to happen twice in *King Lear;* there are instances of characters, like Edgar, who live a double life, as Edgar does when disguised as Poor Tom; metaphoric language that multiplies the meaning of words and phrases, indicating not only what something *is*, but what it is *like*. In Act 3, two tales of suffering amplify the horror of each, a process made possible by the very structure of contrapuntal stagecraft we have been examining. But there is another form of doubleness in *Lear* that we now need to examine in the context of Act 3, the fact that, as we briefly discussed in the Introduction to this book, there are two texts of this play. Sometimes they are essentially congruent, diverging in no significant ways. But in Act 3, they differ in one especially important way, that is, the absence from the Folio text of part of a scene present in the Quarto and printed in the Arden edition as 3.6.17–55. In the opening lines of the scene, present in both Folio and Quarto, Gloucester has led Lear and his bedraggled party to a farmhouse where they intend to sleep before pushing on to Dover. In the Quarto, before Lear sleeps, however, he insists on arraigning his daughters for their cruelty to him. His daughters, of course, are not present except in Lear's imagination, and their arraignment or trial is conducted not in a court of law before a judge and jury, but in the farmhouse before Edgar (disguised as Poor Tom), the Fool and Kent.

This portion of 3.6 is cacophonous in the extreme and depicts a world turned upside down. Justice is mocked as those who sit in judgement on Goneril and Regan speak nonsense or far from the point. Edgar, in doggerel laced with references to contemporary tracts describing the exorcism or casting out of devils, continues his impersonation of Poor Tom; he and the Fool both sing snatches of old songs, probably attempting to distract Lear from his vain pursuit of what he thinks will be justice. Lear, however, will not be deterred as he berates his companions for letting Goneril escape. Only at line 56 do the two versions of the text again begin to overlap as Poor Tom, moved to pity by Lear's distress, pretends to drive away the dogs that Lear believes are barking at him. In this, Edgar displays human kindness aimed at ameliorating the suffering of his brainsick king. Lear's final words in this scene, the mock trial over, are a plea for silence and darkness, even as they indicate the topsy-turvy condition of his mind and of his world: 'Make no noise, make no noise, draw the curtains. So, so, so; we'll go to supper i'the morning so, so, so' (3.6.80–1). To which the Fool adds: 'And I'll go to bed at noon' (3.6.82). If Lear's sense of when to sleep and eat is disordered, the Fool will embrace that disorder and go to bed at an untimely hour. These words show how attentively the Fool has, as always, tracked his master's every word. They affirm his solidarity with that master, even as they call attention to Lear's madness. They are also the last words the Fool speaks in the play. When Gloucester rushes into the farmhouse to announce that Lear must leave at once for Dover or be captured, the Fool seems to get left behind in the rush to bundle Lear onto a litter and depart. Some directors have chosen to have the Fool follow Lear to Dover, lurking at the edges of the action. You might want to ask: what is the significance of the Fool's disappearance from the play if indeed he does disappear after Act 3? What are the advantages, if any, of having him continue to be a stage presence?

I would also invite you to think like a director for a moment for another reason, and that is to consider whether 3.6.17–55 should be omitted from the play text and so from performance. If you consider Act 3 as an orchestrated sequence of scenes, what is gained or lost by the elimination of much of 3.6? Besides indicating something about Lear's mental state, the omitted lines also raise crucial questions about the possibility of earthly justice in the world depicted in *King Lear*, especially because they are part of the prelude to 3.7 and the blinding of Gloucester, which also raises the question of justice. Will anyone punish Cornwall and Regan's vicious cruelty to Gloucester or both Lear's elder daughters for their harsh behaviour towards their father? Is Lear's relentless desire to punish his enemies motivated by a quest for justice or by something else? You might also want to consider whether, in the contrapuntal dramaturgy of this act, the mock trial makes the audience think about the value of small acts of kindness in the face of immense suffering. Who exhibits kindness in this scene? And who exhibits kindness in the scene of Gloucester's blinding? Do such actions matter? Remember that there are no simple answers to these questions. The most satisfying answers, however, grow from full attention to the specifics of the scene and its position in the contrapuntal structure of Act 3.

Redemption twice over?

By the end of Act 3 the storm has passed. In its aftermath the audience or reader gradually absorbs the consequences of the night. Gloucester is now blind, wending his slow way to Dover with Edgar leading him but not revealing who he really is. Edgar still plays Poor Tom, though now he is dressed in peasant clothes that Gloucester's kind tenant has brought him. This sartorial change, like every such change in the play, is potentially charged with meaning. What does it signal? Is Edgar shedding an old disguise and groping towards a new identity? Look for other clues, verbal and visual, that further illuminate Edgar's continuing changes of dress and speech. Simultaneously, while Gloucester and his disguised son move towards Dover, Lear's friends and his daughter Cordelia attempt to rescue and give Lear shelter.

Often, after the central crisis of a tragedy, the protagonist is absent from the stage for a period. When this figure returns, something has frequently changed. Hamlet, for example, having been sent away to England by Claudius in Act 4, returns to Denmark more determined to pursue his revenge against Claudius. But while Lear is absent for the first five scenes of Act 4, when he returns in scene 6, he is simply deeper into his madness, crowned with weeds and raving. Yet even in this desperate state, Lear flickeringly reveals piercing insights into the hypocrisy of the justice system and the corruption of the court world, and in one poignant moment, he even recognizes his old friend, Gloucester. In insanity he sees some things to which he previously had been blind.

The meeting of Gloucester and Lear somewhere in the fields near Dover is one of the iconic moments in the play. They have not seen each other since Gloucester gave shelter to Lear in the farmhouse. At that point Gloucester had eyes and Lear was at the tipping point between madness and sanity. Now the one is blind and the other a lunatic. As we will discuss in much greater detail in the final chapter, when Peter Brook made a film of the play in 1971, he shot it in black and white and set this meeting on a rock-strewn beach. The two old men, the one bloodstained, the other madly crowned with weeds, a 'ruined piece of nature' (4.6.130), sat beside one another in a landscape of utter bleakness. The visual effect was apocalyptic. It was if the end of the world had come. As you read this encounter (4.6.80–183), make a list of some striking elements of the scene that you find particularly important, using all the tools we have been discussing in this or earlier chapters. What words, if any, are emphatically repeated in this encounter? What metaphors help you understand Lear's state of mind and his critique of the world he finds so soiled and full of hypocrisy? You might look at lines 121–5, for example, and think about why he compares women's lower bodies to those of centaurs or to the stinking pit of hell. How does this moment connect to other moments of misogyny in Lear's earlier speeches? How does the centaur image connect to the many other human–animal comparisons in the play?

You might also consider whether Gloucester's speech differs from Lear's in syntax, diction or metaphor. What kind of contrast is being set up between them? Are there any implied stage directions in the scene? For example, when Lear says 'pull off my boots' (4.6.169), is this such a direction? Should Gloucester do it? If he takes this as a command, even if it comes from a madman, how might this act restore something of Gloucester's sense of how the world should work and his position in it? Recall that Gloucester has begged at line 128, 'O, let me kiss that hand!' when he has recognized it is the old King to whom he is speaking. Again, does it matter if Gloucester does physically kiss Lear's hand? Why would this gesture matter to him, and why would Lear insist that his hand must be wiped first, to remove the smell of mortality? In this complex and moving encounter, Gloucester seems to press for a restoration of a relationship he needs and loves; Lear seems to shrink from resuming the kingly position that he now identifies with hypocrisy and corruption. Even Lear's own body is now experienced by him, not as the all-powerful and impregnable monarchical body he once believed he inhabited, but as the decaying flesh of a mere mortal, edging inexorably towards death.

Two striking actions bracket this encounter between the blind Gloucester and the mad Lear, again raising questions about how a contrapuntal dramaturgy, shuttling the viewer or reader between the two plots of the play, affects its meaning and lets us see things that might otherwise go unnoted. In the first part of 4.6 the disguised Edgar, never revealing his true identity, leads his blind father to what he tells him is the top of the Dover cliffs. He arranges a trick whereby his father believes he has leaped from those cliffs and the gods have saved him from death, even though Gloucester has stood on firm ground the whole time. Immediately after that, the mad Lear enters, and the two old men have their interchange. In 4.7, Lear is brought onstage, sleeping, finally having been returned to the care of his daughter Cordelia. He wakes, and they speak.

We have discussed how the two plots of *King Lear* are structurally juxtaposed at many points in the drama. This is true again here. Now the comparison involves, on the one hand, Gloucester and his loyal son, and on the other, Lear and his loyal daughter. Both fathers have been long separated from these children, and in the interim have suffered at the hands of their less kind offspring. Both Edgar and Cordelia seem bent on helping their respective parents, redeeming them from despair and madness. But if you wish to explore more fully why Shakespeare so carefully sets up this comparison, you will want to ask not only what is similar about the two parent–child encounters, but also what is different – different in terms of what the two children wish for their parents and also how they comport themselves. One of the great mysteries of the play, for example, is why Edgar does not reveal himself to his father but instead continues to play roles and assume disguises. After he makes Gloucester believe that Gloucester has survived a fall from the cliff, for example, Edgar pretends to be a man on the beach who saw Gloucester fall from a great height. He also tells Gloucester he saw a fiend with horns and a thousand noses leave the blind man's side (4.6.70–1). Cordelia, by contrast, assumes no disguises, but approaches her father as she is, his daughter. What is the significance of how differently the two children deal with their fathers' suffering and their reconciliations with these respective parents?

To help develop an argument, make a list of other details that you see as potentially important in terms of defining how the two scenes differ, remembering all the ways plays communicate with their readers and audiences. For example, what kinds of speech do the two children use when talking to their parent? How would you characterize the way Edgar addresses his father and how Cordelia addresses hers? What gestures accompany their words? Does either employ elaborate metaphors or word pictures? Or speak with notable plainness? While both speak in verse, does one character or the other use a more regular iambic pentameter line? Does one tend to use words with many syllables as opposed to words with few? Are there any telling stage directions, explicit or implicit, that show how the two parent–child encounters differ? Is the language of clothing used differently in the two scenes? These are all now questions that belong in your interpretive toolkit. They arise from what you have learned about how drama works and conveys meaning. Sometimes a particular question will lead to a dead end, but then another question may spark you to come to a really remarkable conclusion.

For me, Edgar's behaviour in this complicated scene is linked to a tendency observable at other moments in the play when he is overtaken by what I call a 'pedagogical impulse', that is, the desire to teach moral lessons and to sum up the meaning of a complex situation in a tidy way. For example, Edgar opens Act 4 with a soliloquy or solo speech in which he sums up with some assurance that, having lived through the storm and seen the King suffer, he is at the lowest point of his fortunes, has known the worst than can befall him (4.1.1–9). But a moment later Edgar's father, Gloucester, enters the stage, blind. In an aside Edgar says: 'O gods! Who is't can say "I am at the worst"?' (4.1.27). In the scene in which he entices his father to believe he has jumped off a cliff that is not there, Edgar again gives free rein to this same pedagogical impulse, striving to teach Gloucester a lesson about despair and about the gods' care for mankind. In doing so, he uses a battery of theatrical devices: creating a hill by words alone, painting a picture of the dizzying view from the cliff, providing sound effects as he pretends to leave Gloucester, and adopting a new persona as he approaches him on the beach. An interesting question is what Shakespeare might be saying about his own medium, theatre. Is Edgar a clever practitioner, using theatre appropriately? Or are his tactics questionable? Does Shakespeare use the same theatrical skills as Edgar and for the same purposes? When you turn to Cordelia in the ensuing scene, do you believe she shares Edgar's pedagogical impulses? And which of the two children has a more lasting effect on their parent's behaviour or outlook? Does, for example, Gloucester again succumb to despair? Does he continue to believe in the gods' care for humanity? Does Edgar stop designing instructive lessons after the Dover cliff scene, or does he continue to do so?

Writing matters

The prompts below invite you to begin to connect individual observations about aspects of *King Lear* into arguments that make larger claims about some of the big issues that Acts 3 and 4 have brought to your attention. The start of a good argument is always some concrete data and a good question to ask of it. Review some of the topics this chapter has addressed and the questions it has prompted. What have you observed that you want to explore further? Then fashion a question about that material to which your essay will provide an answer. Brainstorm what that productive question might be. For example, a question following from Edgar's attempt to make his father believe he has survived a fall from Dover cliff might be something as simple as: what is Shakespeare's dramatic purpose in having the disguised Edgar deceive his father about his fall from Dover cliff? There are many arguments you could make as an answer to this question, and in developing one of them you will be making an argument about the scene and maybe about its place in the unfolding of the entire drama. You might want to focus on what it says about Edgar; on how characters in the play deal with despair; on whether there are divine powers at work in the world of the play; on how the main and subplots work differently, or similarly; on the play's use of disguise, theatricality or journeys. You cannot address every possible issue these events raise; in fact, your argument will lose focus if you do. Instead, choose a main line of argument and begin building evidence to support that argument from the many observations you have made in your close reading of this dramatic encounter. Then test your hypothesis by asking if there is any evidence that contradicts your central claim. If there is, you may want to change or adjust your argument to take account of these aspects of the text.

Here are some specific prompts that will help you move from observation to argument, using the tools we have developed in this chapter:

1 Choose a group of interrelated metaphors (or similes) that are prominent in Acts 3 and 4 and make an argument about why they are important. We have focused partly on human–animal comparisons, but there are many other metaphors prominent in this part of the play that are used to explain vulnerability, beauty and evil. Decide which metaphors to analyse and fashion a question to which your analysis of those metaphors affords an answer. Organize your evidence to build an argument.

2 Besides the storm, can you identify any other symbolic events, objects or people in Acts 3 or 4? Is the invented persona of Poor Tom such a figure? Is the conversation between Gloucester and Lear in the fields of Dover such an event? How do you know? What evidence would you give for your decision? And what is the function of the symbolic event or figure you have identified?

3 Disguises in the middle part of *King Lear* are not only assumed by Edgar. Kent, for example, pretends to be a simple servant, Caius, after his banishment, and not a nobleman. In this disguise he follows Lear on his long trek from Goneril's castle in Act 1 until the old King dies on the battlefield at the end of Act 5. A question might be: what is the purpose of Kent's disguising himself as a lowly servant? Alternatively, you might ask: does Kent's disguise function the same way as Edgar's? Assemble evidence as you prepare your answer, thinking back over when and how the two men go into disguise, how they use their disguise, and how they emerge from it.

4 In this chapter we discussed scenic juxtapositions in Act 3 and in the two final scenes of Act 4. What can you say about the way scenes are orchestrated or juxtaposed in scenes 1–5 of Act 4? Why, for example, does Albany reappear in the play at this point, and how is his reintroduction framed?

5 Part of 3.6, the lines dealing with the mock trial of Lear's daughters, appear only in the Quarto, as we discussed. Another entire scene, 4.3 in the Arden edition, is also found

only in the Quarto. In it the disguised Kent and a nameless gentleman discuss several matters: why the King of France has gone back to his country, leaving Cordelia behind; how Cordelia has responded to news of her father's suffering; and why the old King won't see Cordelia. What arguments would you make for keeping or deleting this scene? What purpose does it fulfil? How does it function in the context of Act 4 in its entirety? Could it be deleted without loss?

In the next chapter of this book, we will turn to the resolution of *Lear*'s action in the events of Act 5 while examining several of the many memorable films that have created powerful interpretations of the play. In doing so, I hope to show how different performances can realize the play in strikingly dissimilar ways, even as each remains attentive to the work's linguistic and performative potential. To see how that is so, let's go to Act 5 and see what the language of performance can teach us.

CHAPTER THREE

Is This the Promised End?

Preliminaries

This chapter is about endings. How do tragedies end, and how does *King Lear*, in particular, end? When a play's events conclude, does that mean that all the issues it has raised are tidily resolved? In this chapter we are going to highlight some verbal and performance features of the final act of *King Lear* that will help you write well about these questions and about the distinctive aspects of Act 5. In some instances we will be revisiting devices of language (like metaphor, the imperative mode, verbal repetition) or of theatrical construction (like the juxtaposition of scenes) that we have considered previously. However, reading or watching *King Lear* is a cumulative process. Repetition of a particular key word, metaphor or other rhetorical device invites heightened attention to that construction and multiplies the possibilities for making connections across different parts of the play. Some features of Act 5, however, feel unique to its concluding moments, and we will begin with one: the repeated dramatization of dead bodies.

As we have discussed in prior chapters, writing about any part of *King Lear* often works best if it is motivated by close engagement with a particular moment in which you are intensely interested and from which you can then make larger claims. Working with the last act of the play is a great opportunity carefully to choose the topics that will let you make such an argument, one grounded in careful attention to verbal and performance features of the text but that also allows you to develop a comprehensive exploration of some aspect of the play. Perhaps, for example, you will want to pull together moments that address a theme you find important, such as gender injustice, or that employ a particular rhetorical device in distinctive ways.

After examining some specific aspects of the final act of *King Lear*, we will direct our attention at the end of this chapter to two film versions of *King Lear*, one directed by Peter Brook in 1971 and one by Trevor Nunn in 2008. These are strikingly different realizations of and responses to the play. The former was filmed in black and white in the cold and icy landscape of a Jutland winter. The latter was filmed in technicolor and set, not in ancient Britain, but in what has the look and feel of Tsarist Russia in the late nineteenth century. Brook considerably shortened the play text and rearranged the order of some scenes; he also changed details of the staged action. To take one example, in Brook's film Goneril does not poison her sister Regan; instead, Goneril throws Regan to the ground where she dies from the impact. Nunn, by contrast, included much more of the printed text and remained quite faithful to the order of action established in the printed texts of the play. But he also made some strong interpretive choices regarding costume and stage action. By focusing on several of the striking differences in how these two directors staged the final scenes of the play, we can see how they were responding to the text's cues even as they were putting their own interpretive imprint on the performed event. You will have a chance to write about the choices they made when staging Act 5 and about the choices you would make, were you staging or filming this action.

Death and dead bodies

If you ask most people what defines a tragedy, many would say that it is a play that ends in the death of the protagonist. That is true as far as it goes. While in some Greek tragedies the hero lives on beyond the play's conclusion, Shakespeare's tragic heroes do not. In *Lear*, moreover, the old King is not the only one to die. The bodies of all three of his children are on the stage with him at the end of the play; the offstage death of Gloucester has been reported by Edgar; and an attendant comes onstage near the scene's conclusion to say that Edmund also has died. In addition, Kent announces after Lear dies that he must follow his master, which strongly implies that Kent's death is shortly to follow. This litany of the dead does not include, moreover, the many unnamed soldiers who have died in the battle that took place somewhere offstage in 5.2. It is not an exaggeration to say that *Lear*'s ending has a mortuary feel. Remember that in the first scene of the play Lear had renounced his active kingship so that he could 'unburdened crawl toward death' (1.1.40). As it turns out, *death* becomes a keyword of the play, one sometimes opposed, as we will see, to *life*. As the play unfolds, however, Lear's opening statement of intention proves both prescient and wrong. The old King does travel towards death, but he does not so much crawl as struggle towards it, his passage made tortuous by the elements; by the unkind acts of his daughters, and of Cornwall and Edmund; and by his own inner torment, rage and shame. The journey towards death does not prove to be the untroubled glide path the old King had envisioned.

As an indication of how hard this passage towards death will be, from the moment that Lear sets out from his castle for his first sojourn with his eldest daughter, the play shows him perpetually in motion, journeying, journeying, often in desperate and uncomfortable circumstances. He crosses the barren heath on horseback, in a litter and on foot, moving sometimes with almost no attendants between the castles of Goneril, Regan and Gloucester, the hovel where he meets Poor Tom, and the farmhouse where he arraigns his older daughters in a parody of justice before being carried off towards Dover. This haphazard journey, literalized on the stage by the old King's frantic struggles against the storm and his many arrivals and departures from the entryways of hovels and castles, has as its telos the geographical end point of Dover. Dover is the play's gravitational lodestone, pulling all the action and all the play's characters towards itself. It is the part of Britain nearest France from which Cordelia comes with her army and the part of Britain distinguished by the famous white cliffs from which Gloucester hopes to cast himself to his death. It is at Dover, then, that the deaths of so many characters occur, including Lear's. While the old King foretold his end in scene 1.1, he could never have predicted the journey he would take before finally arriving at his destination.

It is important to note how many of these Act 5 deaths actually occur offstage. We know characters have died because their bodies are carried onto the stage as corpses, enacting the perpetually paradoxical phenomenon of live actors playing dead people. But the actual event of dying onstage is reserved for Lear. You might ask why and might sketch out some first thoughts as to why the deaths at the end of the play are handled as they are. For example, why do we not see Gloucester, Lear's daughters, or even Edmund, at the actual moment of their deaths? Why, however, does the lead-up to Edmund's offstage death after his combat with his disguised brother get so much stage time while we are denied seeing the crucial reunion between Gloucester and Edgar before Gloucester's heart 'burst smilingly' (5.3.198)? Is the playwright making a statement about whose death is most important? Or directing audience attention towards those figures whose impending deaths reveal in them the greatest capacity for change and insight? Or is a focus on the capacity for change a sentimental hope that the play denies as often as it rewards? Death is a threshold moment in the play, long anticipated by some, but visiting others with unexpected celerity, cutting off the young as well as the old. What does Shakespeare's dramatization of death, onstage and off, reveal to us about its possible significance or its approach as a catalyst for insight and change? Death may be a universal phenomenon, but in *King Lear* not all deaths are dramatized in the same way, nor are they all experienced the same way by the audience. We will inevitably return to questions of death and of life as we work through some key moments in Act 5, but at this point you might want to jot down your immediate thoughts about how and why various deaths are dramatized as they are in the play's ending moments.

Dramatic structure: creating an ending

Earlier in this book we talked about scenic juxtapositions as a language of the stage through which particular effects are created. Through much of *Lear*, scenes involving Gloucester and his sons are counterpointed to scenes involving Lear and his daughter, and Gloucester's trek to Dover is set against Lear's precipitous departure from Gloucester's farmhouse, inviting implicit comparisons between the events in the two plots. Act 5 sustains the pattern of comparison through juxtaposition, while also suturing the two plots more closely together. To help you see how the dramatic action takes shape, make a scene chart of how the events of the play's final three scenes are orchestrated, including when the stage is emptied and then restocked with figures. You will quickly see that the first two scenes of Act 5 are comprised of a number of short encounters. In 5.1, Edmund speaks to Regan before the battle; then Goneril and Albany arrive with their soldiers; then Edgar dressed as a peasant brings Albany Goneril's incriminating letter; then Edgar abruptly departs; and Edmund enters to urge Albany to the battle before speaking one of his powerful monologues aimed directly at the audience: a speech boasting about his amatory conquest of both Lear's elder daughters. The whole scene is seventy lines long with many exits and entrances. The second scene, a mere eleven lines, shows Edgar leading Gloucester to shelter under a tree before the final battle, and then depicts Edgar returning to drag his father to another place of safety after Lear's forces have lost.

You might ask: what is the effect of these short, swiftly changing encounters? Clearly, their brevity suggests haste and urgency. Conflict is coming to a head, and characters are making alliances and expressing intentions on the fly. The effect is one of confusion and an accelerating sense of impending danger. Second, the events in the Gloucester and the Lear plots are becoming more intertwined, even though the fates of Lear and Gloucester, Cordelia and Edgar, Edmund and Lear's elder daughters continue to be set in implicit contrast. But now, Edgar is moving from exile towards incorporation into the political order and so closer to the throne and to Lear, reasserting his family's status as loyal followers of the old King. Edgar's long journey back from his outcast state began when, as he headed out to Dover with his blind father, he put on the simple peasant clothes brought to him by his father's servant. Though to Gloucester he still presents himself as the madman, Poor Tom, a figure defined by his near nakedness, to the audience Edgar now looks like a peasant helping a blind man stumble towards Dover. Eventually, this same Edgar will be further transformed when he appears after the battle as a noble challenger to his brother Edmund. How Edgar dresses in that final battle is something to which we will return, but for now simply note how Edgar's movement from outcast to a candidate for the throne of Britain is marked by his successive sartorial transformations. Throughout, clothing acts as a language through which certain meanings are expressed. In Edgar's case, his changes of clothing, or the absence of clothing, signal to the audience his social transformations: both his original loss of identity and status, and his slow ascent back up the social ladder to reincorporation within his family and the political nation.

Another thing to note about the first two short scenes of Act 5 is the stage direction, '*drum and colours*', with which each is introduced. Like dress, the controlled sounds of musical instruments directing the movement of soldiers, and the visual display of flags or colours signifying the group identity of particular troops, are part of the language of performance. The stage direction about drum and colours is also repeated after 5.1.16 when Albany and Goneril enter with their soldiers. Colours are the military banners that are carried into battle; drums, of course, are played as soldiers march into the fray. Immediately after these stage directions, first Edmund, then Albany, and finally Lear pass onto or over the stage with their forces. The sounds and sights indicated by these directions convey information, most obviously that a crucial battle is pending, a battle that will involve everyone. They also call attention to the fact that Edmund and Albany really head two armies that arrive separately and are under two commanding officers, creating, as proves to be true, the possibility that these two leaders might quarrel with one another once they have defeated Cordelia and Lear's combined French and British forces. This impression of two allied armies that are not entirely unified would be underscored if the colours under which Edmund and Albany are marching display not a single insignia, but two different ones.

These scenes contain another important aural cue. After line 4 of 5.2, the stage direction says: '*Alarum and retreat within. Enter* EDGAR.' This single stage direction indicates that the battle for Britain has occurred, but entirely out of the audience's sight. All we hear are the trumpet calls that signal to soldiers that they are to advance or retreat. This stage direction is an example of *synecdoche*, a rhetorical device in which the part of something stands for the whole. Here, the martial signals that the audience hears are a synecdoche for the rest of the unseen battle in Dover's fields. The consequences of the battle are suggested by the urgency with which Edgar rushes back to where he has deposited Gloucester in order to drag him away again. The people on the losing side are in danger. But why stage the battle in this truncated fashion? One answer might be a purely practical one: the difficulty of staging a convincing battle scene that would require many actors. This seems unlikely, however, to be the chief concern because Shakespeare's company staged a number of plays at the Globe that required such scenes. Rather, the reduction of the actual battle to some trumpet signals suggests that the battle itself is not Shakespeare's primary focus. Instead, the play draws the audience's attention towards what happens as a *result* of this battle, and the consequences are not what the audience might have expected. First, if audience members or readers had encountered the older versions of the Lear story, they might expect the old King and Cordelia to survive this battle and even perhaps for Cordelia to marry Edgar. Those expectations are defeated. Moreover, when Edgar proclaims to his blind father that he must flee because Lear's forces have lost, one might expect that we would see the complete conquest of the King's party and the ultimate triumph of Edmund, whose surging theatrical energy far eclipses that of Albany. Instead, at the end of the play, Edmund and his two love interests, Goneril and Regan, are dead; and only forces loyal to Lear hold the stage: Albany, Edgar and Kent. In a series of ironic reversals, the winners of the battle become the losers, though Lear does not experience this reversal as a triumph. As you continue to think about how this tragedy ends, what would you say about the reversal whereby the defeat of Cordelia's army does not lead to the victory of her opponents? Is our sense of justice served by this turn of events? Is it possible to feel the ending is just if Cordelia nonetheless is executed? You will have opportunities to comment on this question further below.

The final scene of Act 5 is a long one of 325 lines. It is through the events of this scene that the play comes to rest. It begins with another '*drum and colours*' stage direction, but this time that stage direction is not a call to battle but an accompaniment to Lear and Cordelia's journey to prison. The major events of this last scene include Lear and Cordelia's conversation as they are led to confinement, the battle between Edgar and Edmund, and Lear's arrival onstage with Cordelia's dead body. We will dig into all three of these events using the tools of analysis we have been developing over the course of this book, attending not just to how the plot ends, but to how the play's concluding movement makes the reader or audience member think harder about key issues such as the possibility of earthly justice and of the equitable distribution of resources, humankind's proper relationship to the earth and to all the creatures that inhabit it, and the competition between altruism and self-interest that is everywhere apparent in the play. Some of these issues are explored in tandem, creating a dense web of interconnected ideas.

The languages and institutions of justice

Throughout our investigation of *King Lear*, questions of justice have loomed large. Take a moment to recall some of the dramatic moments when these questions have been underscored. For example, in the first scenes of the play, Lear's rashness and Gloucester's thoughtless gullibility prompt questions about whether they treat their children justly, not only their 'good' children whom they cast out, but those offspring the play invites us to see as deeply flawed: Edmund, Goneril and Regan. Is Lear's demand that his daughters love him 'all' a just demand? Is Gloucester's treatment of Edmund 'just' when he penalizes him for a bastardy that is not his fault and makes jokes about his conception? In their turns, do Goneril and Regan and Edmund act justly when, perhaps partly as a result of ill treatment, they subject their fathers to physical and mental torment of remarkable severity? Do both Lear and Gloucester come to see their own responsibility for a more just and equitable distribution of material wealth and immaterial love, and do they act on those insights? You might recall Lear's speech before he enters the hovel in Act 3 when he empathizes with the suffering of the 'poor naked wretches' (3.4.28) who are exposed to the storm. At that point he vows to 'Take physic, pomp' (3.4.33) and show the heavens more just by his own acts of redistribution, implying that he has previously failed to tend justly to the needs of his subjects and to fulfil his obligations to them.

This thought finds an echo in the words of the blind Gloucester when, giving his purse to Poor Tom for leading him to Dover, he says: 'So distribution should undo excess / And each man have enough' (4.1.73–4). Gloucester's entire speech, which you might want to revisit, echoes biblical injunctions to give to the poor to avoid God's wrath and to accrue spiritual treasure in heaven. The religious injunction to practise charity as a way to create justice on earth might be compared to Lear's more political articulation of the need for the powerful, those who rule, to attend to the material needs of their subjects as part of a system of mutual obligation. While Lear's words express a paternalistic sense of the privileged giving their 'superflux' (3.4.35) or excess to their subjects, rather than advocating a radical sharing of all earthly resources and treasure, Lear nonetheless articulates in the storm his own political and moral obligations to those below him in the hierarchical social order he takes for granted. This is a riposte not only to his own self-centredness but to his prior obliviousness to his obligations as king and father. Is there any evidence from later in the play that suggests Lear *acts on* this recognition of his responsibility for acts of redistribution?

When he goes mad, Lear's thoughts harp repeatedly on the theme of the injustices that he feels have been done to him by his daughters. In Gloucester's farmhouse he enacts a wild mock version of one of the chief institutions of justice: the trial. In 3.6, Lear imagines calling Regan and Goneril to account for their crimes against him, summoning the Fool, Edgar as Poor Tom, and even Kent, to play a part in this farcical enactment of a trial. The irony of the scene cuts in several possible directions. Who or what does it discredit? Do you think it makes Lear and his companions look foolish for pretending to be judges and for calling an imaginary Goneril to account? Or does the mock trial call into question the fairness of actual courts as sites of justice? Lear at a later point excoriates the hypocrisy and unfairness of those charged with administering justice when he speaks with Gloucester on the beach at Dover. In one part of his furious rant at officers of justice, he says:

> a dog's
> obeyed in office.
> Thou, rascal beadle, hold thy bloody hand;
> Why dost thou lash that whore? Strip thine own back,
> Thou hotly lusts to use her in that kind
> For which thou whipp'st her. The usurer hangs the cozener.
> Through tattered clothes great vices do appear;
> Robes and furred gowns hide all. Plate sin with gold,
> And the strong lance of justice hurtless breaks;
> Arm it in rags, a pigmy's straw does pierce it.
> None does offend, none, I say none.

(4.6.154–64)

This wonderful, wrathful speech is a slashing indictment of the inequal treatment of rich and poor, privileged and powerless, before the law. What devices make this speech effective? Make your own list, beginning, perhaps, with 'A dog's obeyed in office.' What makes this a powerful sentence? Is it the surprising thought that an animal might hold an office usually reserved for humans? Is it that the dog in this sentence is a placeholder for a corrupt figure of juridical authority so that such a person is implicitly being compared to a dog? Is it, perhaps, the disconcerting possibility that a dog in office might wear human robes of justice? Does this statement equalize men and dogs or hierarchize them? Does it lower or raise the reader's estimation of people invested with worldly authority?

This sentence ushers in a series of lines in which surprising reversals, many involving clothing, are articulated. What are some of those reversals, and how do they connect to image patterns we have examined elsewhere in this book? The corrupt officer of justice, for example, is enjoined to strip his back, to become partly naked and afflicted by the lashes of a whip. Here the language of clothing again points up discrepancies in the treatment of rich and poor. We do not expect an officer of the law to be whipped; his office protects him, while all too often those who are branded whores by the legal system are readily assumed to be worthy of such devastating punishment. Successive lines imply that if one wears furred gowns, or golden adornments, which are signs of privilege, the weapons of the law will never touch that person, no matter how unjust such differential treatment may be. But if a sinner wears only rags, it takes nothing stronger than a piece of straw wielded by a pigmy for that person to become subject to the 'lance' (4.6.162) of the law – lance being a word meaning a weapon and also an action: to cut the flesh. Justice wounds only the poor, Lear implies. Throughout this speech, differences in size image forth differences in power, as do contrasts between clothing and nakedness. As a result, Lear, in his madness (or is it in a moment of heightened sanity?) proclaims: 'None does offend, none' (4.6.164), imagining for a moment a world in which crime and punishment are erased since the inequities within society make it impossible for justice to be achieved. Do you think the play as a whole is as sceptical about the possibility of justice as Lear appears to be here? Give your reasons and the evidence to support your point of view.

You might want to consider if there are any moments in the play when justice seems to prevail. If so, how are they brought about? The play's rich explorations of these questions is woven through nearly every scene of the play, including 5.3. It is to that scene that I now ask you to turn your attention, especially to that part that introduces a new institution of justice: the trial by combat between Edgar and Edmund. This event, with the extended exchanges that form its immediate aftermath, stretches from line 82 to line 254. The trial by combat it depicts is an ancient method of determining who is in the right in a legal dispute. Rather than justice being rendered by a judge or a jury, two combatants agree to fight one another until one of them is defeated. The victor is presumed to have justice on their side. Trials by combat were highly ritualized affairs usually taking place in the lists, a square area marked off to delimit the place of combat, and they involved each combatant agreeing to rules of battle. In Shakespeare's plays, the most famous trial by combat *almost* occurs in the opening act of *Richard II* when two enemies, Mowbray and Henry Bolingbroke, are called to the lists to engage in battle to settle a dispute between them. But King Richard suddenly stops the contest before it starts, truncating and undermining this ritualized form of determining justice. The trial by combat in *King Lear* is also somewhat irregular since, while Albany and Edmund have both thrown down their gauntlets as a signal that they or their seconds will engage in a fight, and while a trumpeter three times has blown his instrument to summon a challenger to come to the lists to fight Edmund in Albany's place, when Edgar appears, he will not give his name. 'O know,' he says, 'my name is lost' (5.3.119). As Goneril points out later, Edgar's refusal to give his name could have been an excuse for Edmund not to accept his challenge.

The encounter also raises questions about how Edgar is apparelled. In leading Gloucester to Dover, Edgar wore peasant's garb. When he kills Oswald, he might well have taken a sword from him, but how does he accomplish the 'fair and warlike' appearance Edmund attributes to him in line 140? Does Edgar create the impression of nobility primarily by the way he carries his body and by the elegance of his rhetoric, or has he acquired a full suit of armour and other sartorial markers of nobility somewhere on the battlefield? Consider the implications of both staging decisions. What would it mean if Edgar were now completely returned to the sartorial station he once inhabited before Edmund engineered his banishment? What would it mean, given the play's many disguises, its critique of sartorial luxury and its emphasis on the kindness of those placed low on the social totem pole, if Edgar appears on the battlefield in a costume that does not immediately signal his privileged birth? Should he appear, as often happens, in a ragged and homespun approximation of battle gear? These questions indicate the many important interpretive choices that any director or reader of this play must make. In *Lear* you might want to recall that many of the play's most moving acts of kindness and of redress for injustice are undertaken by the powerless or those who have assumed the persona of such a figure: Edgar as Poor Tom supporting Gloucester on the road to Dover; the Fool sticking with Lear through the storm; the Earl of Kent assuming the guise of a lowly serving man after he has been banished in order to stay with his master; the servant of Cornwall who tries to stop Cornwall from plucking out Gloucester's second eye; the servants on Gloucester's own estate who bring the whites of eggs to cleanse their old master's wounded eyes. There is precedent, then, for imagining that the challenger who comes to do combat with Edmund and bring him to justice might not be wearing the furnishings of a nobleman.

Edgar's confrontation with Edmund, through which his name and social position are again established, is supposed to indicate which man has justice on his side. Edmund's defeat thus suggests that he is indeed a traitor to his king and disloyal to his father and brother. For his part Edgar is quick to attribute the outcome of the combat to the gods and uses it, further, to affirm that his father, Gloucester, justly suffered the loss of his eyes because of his adultery with Edmund's mother:

> The gods are just and of our pleasant vices
> Make instruments to plague us:
> The dark and vicious place where thee he [Gloucester] got
> Cost him his eyes.
>
> (5.3.168–71)

This is a view to which the dying Edmund assents.

How do you respond to this speech? Do you agree that Gloucester has been punished by the gods for a sexual transgression? What evidence could you offer to support your answer? You might want to think back to the assurance that Edgar gives Gloucester that Gloucester has been saved by the gods after his (non-existent) fall from Dover cliff. Does Edgar have a pattern of attributing to the gods what might well have a more human cause? In this play, do the gods guarantee justice, or do human beings? Is this another instance of Edgar's pedagogical impulse, his desire to make all events into a morality tale with a clear message?

There is one further irony that the structure of this scene drives home. When Edmund and Edgar have been reconciled, Kent's arrival, seeking for Lear on the battlefield, makes everyone realize that, while the trial by combat has been occurring, no one has remembered the fate of the old King and of Cordelia. Edmund, meaning for once to do good, reveals that he has ordered them both killed and sends his sword as proof that he wants to rescind his order. As Edmund is carried offstage, a stage direction reads: '*Enter* LEAR *with* CORDELIA *in his arms* [*followed by the* Gentleman]' (s.d. following 5.3.254). While Edgar has been pressing home his claims that the gods are just, Cordelia has been being hung. How does the structure of this scene invite you to interpret this final moment? How does it contribute to the play's complex exploration of the possibilities of a just universe, of just gods, of human beings as agents of justice?

Why should a dog, a horse, a rat have life?

Animals, as we have seen, everywhere populate the imaginative and actual landscape of *King Lear*, and it is partly through thinking about animals that the play expands questions of justice to include a consideration of humanity's relation to and treatment of the creaturely world in which humans are embedded. On the heath and in the farmhouse, humans are literally brought near to the world of animals, both wild and domestic. In some productions and film versions of the play, when Lear takes shelter in Gloucester's farmhouse, for example, he seems to share the space with cows and sheep who occupy covered pens that protect them as well as Lear from the storm. In Peter Brook's film version of the play, the heath scenes include shots of the bodies of dead animals, what look like weasels or badgers, swept up against the brush in the midst of a torrential downpour. They do not look so different from the naked body of Poor Tom, hunched in a ball in a vain attempt to ward off the force of the elements. Film allows the literalization of animals' ubiquity in a way the stage less easily can, but the language of the play forces an encyclopedic array of animals into the reader's consciousness. People are again and again compared to animals, which elicits questions: *are* humans different from other animals? If so, *how* are they different? What can other animals show humans about productive ways to live? What do humans owe to the other creatures with whom they share the earth? How does humans' language often appropriate animals for metaphoric purposes?

To take up these questions a final time, consider three moments in the final scene of *King Lear*. The first is Lear's speech to Cordelia as they are about to be led away to prison. She, aware of the larger family and political context in which they are enmeshed, asks if she and Lear should not see Goneril and Regan. To which Lear replies:

> No, no, no, no. Come, let's away to prison;
> We two alone will sing like birds i'th cage.
> When thou dost ask me blessing I'll kneel down
> And ask of thee forgiveness. So we'll live
> And pray, and sing, and tell old tales, and laugh
> At gilded butterflies, and hear poor rogues
> Talk of court news; and we'll talk with them too –
> Who loses and who wins, who's in, who's out –
> And take upon's the mystery of things
> As if we were God's spies. And we'll wear out
> In a walled prison packs and sects of great ones
> That ebb and flow by the moon.
>
> (5.3.8–19)

The speech opens with Lear's emphatic refusal to engage with his daughters and, as it turns out, with the world in general. His 'no, no, no, no' (5.3.8) recalls earlier moments when Lear refused to face a necessary truth, and it is a direct contradiction of the wishes of the daughter whose words he also refused to harken to in the opening scene of the play. Of course, much is also different from that opening scene. Lear now imagines a perpetual performance of mutuality between his daughter and himself. She will ask for his paternal blessing, and he will ask for her forgiveness for the wrongs he did her. The speech is seductive in that it seems to offer a picture of a changed Lear, one who eschews public power for an intense personal relationship with a beloved daughter.

Focus, however, on the simile that follows Lear's initial vehement refusal to see his older daughters. Lear says that he and Cordelia will 'sing like birds i'th cage' (5.3.9). In projecting a future in which he and Cordelia will sing together like their avian counterparts, Lear implies that the caged bird sings from happiness – else why would Lear compare his own desired future state to that of these caged creatures? Is the bird's song, however, necessarily an expression of happiness rather than a lament or a protest against confinement? Why *should* a bird live in a cage? Who put it there? While the bird is clearly not the focus of Lear's attention, but only a convenient image for him to appropriate in making a certain case to Cordelia, a reader attentive to the bird and animal imagery that permeates the play may be made uneasy by Lear's assumptions about a captured bird's happiness.

Further, the incommensurability between the image of the birdcage and the grim reality of confinement in a prison indicates that Lear may not yet have taken complete stock of his circumstances and that his wish for a safe haven may be a pipedream. The image of the birdcage is disconcerting in other ways. It not only assumes that a bird enjoys confinement, which is likely as much projection as fact, but that so will he and Cordelia. In this simile, in which Lear takes the bird's condition, and its song, as the equivalent of his confined state with Cordelia and of their mutual 'song' of blessing and forgiveness, the old King uses a striking figure of speech to project his will and his wishes onto his daughter. But will she really sing with happiness in this cage? If so, why did she ask to see her sisters, and why does she have a husband if, when all is said and done, she is still to love her father all, and if their mutual gestures of affection and respect are to be her entire world? Confined and happy, happy because confined, happy because completely bound up with her father – this is how Lear defines Cordelia's future through his bird in a cage simile.

If we take this speech as one measure of how much Lear has changed from the first scene of the play, what would you conclude? If Lear was wrong to divide his kingdom and shake off the cares of office prematurely, is he still wrong in his refusal to face 'these sisters and these daughters' (5.3.7), the partial agents of his present plight and of his kingdom's well-being? Or is he right to concentrate mainly on his renewed relationship with his youngest daughter and on their precious moments together? A few lines later Lear suggests that in prison he and Cordelia will laugh at the court world whose inhabitants now seem to him like 'gilded butterflies' (5.3.13) (another implied metaphor drawing on the beauty and supposed gauzy insubstantiality of butterflies to disparage trivial courtiers). In his projected court world, power ebbs and flows in a perpetual state of flux. By contrast, the 'walled prison' (5.3.18) figures in Lear's thought as a place of constancy, joy and safety. But is he right? Are there any safe havens in this play's world, any escape from flux and mutability? Again, note what follows this speech. Edmund orders Lear and Cordelia to be taken away and then orders a captain to kill them. The birdcage does not prove perdurable, and the juxtaposition of Lear's speech with Edmund's creates a dreadful irony. There is a certain cruelty in the last scenes of *Lear*, a harrowing oscillation between hope and despair, the promise of justice and the dashing of that promise. Does this oscillation mean that the quest for justice is without value? This is one of the most difficult questions the play engages.

The nameless Captain Edmund solicits to kill Lear and Cordelia is quite happy to do an unjust act, and he accepts his task in language that again plays upon the supposed differences between men and beasts. To Edmund the Captain replies: 'I cannot draw a cart, nor eat dried oats. / If it be man's work, I'll do't' (5.3.39–40). Implicitly, the Captain compares himself to an animal, probably a horse, in order to suggest how humans and beasts differ. If beasts' role is to pull carts in man's service and to eat grain, not cooked foodstuffs, humankind's role is to do the work proper to man. What is that work? In the logic of the Captain's speech to Edmund, it is the killing of other men. The Captain assumes that beasts exist to serve humans and are inferior to them because humans have higher tasks to perform. But when those higher tasks turn out to be the slaughter of a young woman and an old man without an arraignment or judicial warrant, the assumption of humanity's superiority is at best called in question. But what *is* the proper work of a man if it is not just to be the swift obliteration of creatures of his own kind?

The final dramatic sequence I want to address involving an animal–human comparison occurs when Lear appears onstage with Cordelia in his arms. Throughout the last seventy lines of the play, Lear struggles against the fact of Cordelia's death. He calls for a looking glass to see if her breath might, though imperceptible to him, leave a trace on the mirror's surface; he calls for a feather with the same hope that its movement might register the faint coming and going of breath. At line 304, Lear emits these agonizing lines:

> And my poor fool is hanged. No, no, no life!
> Why should a dog, a horse, a rat have life
> And thou no breath at all? O thou'lt come no more.
> Never, never, never, never, never.
>
> (5.3.304–7)

The 'poor fool' here probably means Cordelia, but the words recall the play's actual Fool, left behind when Lear was suddenly borne away from Gloucester's farmhouse. The Fool's death is assumed and sometimes staged by directors, but in the text the ambiguity in the reference to the hanging of the Fool can cause the audience's attention to flicker for a moment between the two possible referents. Together, the deaths of Cordelia and of the Fool represent a significant portion of the collateral damage caused by the old King's titanic folly in Act 1. As we have noted, the two roles can even, in theory, be played by a single actor, though that seldom happens in modern performances. The word *fool*, however, evokes a double presence, a double sorrow, a double loss. It draws the audience's attention back to Lear's faithful companion in the first three acts of the play even as it focuses attention on the corpse of Cordelia now on the stage. As Lear scrutinizes his daughter's body, his speech returns to patterns of repetition and enumeration with which we are familiar but that in this context convey new meaning. Consider the verbal repetition of 'No, no, no life!' (5.3.304) and 'Never, never, never, never, never' (5.3.307). What effects do these lines create? What prior lines and words do they recall? How does the repetition of the 'n' sound work within each line and then between them? What syllables are accented? You may well want to write about these lines, thinking back to other moments when Lear and other characters used similar words, including the play on *nothing* that is so important to the play's opening act.

In the final act of the play you will recall that, when Lear refused to see his elder daughters after his defeat by their armies, his exclamation of 'No, no, no, no' (5.3.8) served as a refusal, a proclamation that he would not do as Cordelia wished and see his other offspring. But in the passage we are discussing, 'no, no, no' (5.3.304) modifies *life*. It is an adjective that, through its relentless iteration, conveys Lear's despair at the finality of Cordelia's death. She has no life at all, none. The *Oxford English Dictionary* suggests that in the early modern period life could mean simply 'animate existence', but it could also mean 'something which represents the cause or source of living or of vitality; a vivifying or animating principle; . . . "soul"; "essence".' These meanings are all present in Lear's lines: Cordelia now lacks the animating principle, the soul or essence, that gave her being its vital force and that sustained not only her, but also her old father.

As opposed, then, to the deaths that proliferate at the end of this play, Lear's search for a sign of his daughter's life reveals his desperate dependency on her vital essence to sustain his own will to live. In Genesis 2.9, the King James Bible describes humanity's creation in this way: 'And the Lord God formed man of the dust of the ground, and breathed into his nostrils the breath of life; and man became a living soul.' Jacobean readers and theatregoers were accustomed to hearing the Bible read from the pulpit; many were used to reading the Bible themselves. They might well have remembered this verse as Lear searches for his daughter's breath. Remember that, when Lear first awakened from his long madness and saw his daughter Cordelia before him, he said that she must be 'a soul in bliss' (4.7.46), meaning that her soul had been transported from earth to heaven after her death. But, of course, Cordelia had not died at that point, and the breath that animated her body in that scene issued from a living self. Now Cordelia has become a corpse, and Lear can perceive no signs of her vital essence: no breath, no life. The finality of the five repetitions of the word *never* raises the possibility that perhaps neither on earth nor in heaven will Lear again be in the presence of Cordelia. There is no mention here of souls in bliss. Do you think that the ending of the play forecloses the possibility of an afterlife, either pagan or Christian? What argument would you make about this difficult question? Remember to root your thoughts in an engagement with the play's language and dramatic structure.

One further line invites attention. Lear asks: 'Why should a dog, a horse, a rat have life / And thou no breath at all?' (5.3.305–6). Lear's question assumes that a person's life, while circumstances may make it cheap as a beast's, *should* be of greater value than that of dog, horse or rat. Accustomed as we are to thinking of human exceptionality and of the special value of human life, we may well agree with Lear at this moment. Why, indeed, should dogs, horses and rats – these so-called subhuman creatures – still have the breath of life when Cordelia does not? However, the play has already queried whether the lives of people and of other creatures should be weighed against one another in quite this way, through simple assertions of humanity's greater value. In this play the difference between man and man is great, the relative superiority of beasts to men has, in some contexts, been called into question, particularly in the storm scenes and through the person of Poor Tom. What motivates Lear's question here, of course, is an overwhelming sense of injustice. Why should the daughter upon whom he has fixed his love be dead while mere dogs have life? But as Lear moves towards his own end, and the play's, we might ask if the injustice visited on Cordelia did not spring in part from the reflexive sense of superiority that assumes the dominion of humans over other animals, and of some humans over others? Edmund had Cordelia killed, but the impetus for her death had its origins in the love test of the play's first scene. Sitting at the pinnacle of his society, Lear assumed that his position meant that no one really mattered but himself. He took too little care of the feelings and the necessarily divided loyalties of his grown daughters, too little care of loyal subjects like Kent, too little care of those whose lives were lived among the beasts of the fields. If the universe is to be rebalanced, we may feel, the arrogance that makes the privileged cling to notions of their superiority to all the creatures with which they cohabit the earth must be given over, whether those be dogs, rats, horses, daughters, base peasants or Poor Toms. In our own day and time, this may be one of the most important possible meanings of this ever-evolving tragedy.

The vagaries of the imperative

One particular verb form – the imperative – marked many of Lear's early and most memorable statements. From the opening scene he frequently commanded others to speak: 'Goneril, / Our eldest born, speak first' (1.1.54); or to Cordelia, 'How, nothing will come of nothing. Speak again' (1.1.90). He ordered others to harken to him as when he says to Kent: 'Hear me, recreant, on thine allegiance, hear me' (1.1.168). He ordered the winds to blow at his command: 'Blow, winds and crack your cheeks! Rage, blow!' (3.2.1), and he ordered the gods to make Goneril sterile: 'Hear, Nature, hear, dear goddess, hear: / Suspend thy purpose if thou didst intend / To make this creature fruitful' (1.4.267–9). After he wakes from his great madness in the presence of Cordelia in 4.7, his speech patterns change. In that dialogue with his daughter (4.7.44–84), Lear speaks mostly in simple declarative sentences 'I am a very foolish, fond old man' (4.7.60) or asks straightforward questions: 'Be your tears wet?' (4.7.71). Most of his word choices are monosyllables. But when he later urges Cordelia to come away to prison with him, the imperative, 'Come' (5.3.8), reappears in the first line of his speech, signally perhaps a persistent assumption that he can still determine his daughter's choices and movements. The rest of the speech is the descriptive reverie on the blissful life the two of them will lead during their incarceration that we discussed above.

Now examine for yourself what happens to the imperative verb form after Lear returns with Cordelia in his arms at 5.3.254. Read through to the end of the play and note who uses imperatives and in what context. Does Lear? Do Edgar, Kent or Albany? I have always found it very moving when Kent, seeing that Lear has fainted after his final words to Cordelia's body says: 'Break, heart, I prithee break' (5.3.311). This is a command delivered to a bodily organ, Lear's heart, willing it to cease beating. Interestingly, the first word of command, 'Break', is followed by something closer to an entreaty, 'I prithee break.' Seemingly stern words of command modulate into a final expression of love. Kent would not have Lear suffer any further. Edgar, however, interjects: 'Look up, my lord' (311), the imperative mode comprising a command for Lear to live whether he wishes to or not. This act of perhaps understandable selfishness Kent immediately reproves: 'Vex not his ghost; O, let him pass' (312). In Peter Brook's version of the scene, Edgar speaks his line while bending over Lear and trying to rouse him. Kent, however, roughly throws Edgar off Lear's body, preventing Edgar's attempts at prolonging the old King's life. You might want to consider further the various ways in which the imperative form is used in the final moments of the play: by whom, for what, with what emotional impact?

Strikingly, Lear's final lines also employ the imperative mode, but to mysterious effect. After he has asked to have a button loosened,

Lear speaks for the last time: 'Do you see this? Look on her: look, her lips, / Look there, look there! *He dies*' (5.3.309–10). Part of the mystery of these lines is that it is not clear to whom Lear is speaking. It could be to Edgar, who speaks next; or to Kent who in performance is often placed close to Lear and is often the one who undoes his button. Could Lear be speaking to himself? But what is Lear commanding his ambiguous addressee to behold? A clue may lie in the reference to Cordelia's lips. It is from those lips that both Cordelia's breath and speech issued when she was alive. At this moment, does Lear believe he sees the breath of life still issuing from those lips? If so, his heart, like Gloucester's, might be breaking from joy at the thought his daughter still lives. Or does he believe he sees her soul leaving her body, that she has died but may become that soul in bliss he believed her to be when he woke from his madness? In a number of productions, Lear casts his eyes up to the heavens as he speaks his last lines, as if following the upward progress of her soul. If so, what emotions might that elicit from him? Or, when Lear looks on Cordelia's lips, does he simply see nothing: no movement, no life, no essence, no soul? Is he calling another person to witness the unspeakable bleakness of that fact, at which his heart finally does break, but not from joy? You might well want to write about this moment, making an argument about why these are Lear's final lines. What sense of an ending do they convey? How would you stage them to best express their meaning and emotional tonality?

Making an ending: *Lear* as film

There are many film versions of *King Lear*, and they all handle the ending of the play differently. A comparative approach allows what is distinctive about different versions to emerge. As I indicated earlier, Peter Brook's 1971 black-and-white film starring Paul Scofield approaches the Lear story very differently from Trevor Nunn's 2008 film featuring Ian McKellen in the title role. I encourage you to seek out both versions (see the brief filmography at the end of the annotated bibliography) and to watch them in their entirety. Together they reveal how two experienced directors respond to Shakespeare's play as the jumping-off point for their own acts of interpretation and creation. Resist judging these films primarily in terms of their faithfulness to the Shakespearean text. They are independent works of art, but each may provoke you to think further about what you found challenging and moving in Shakespeare's play and what you yourself want to emphasize as you write about it. Film, of course, is a different medium from theatre, and were you to write extensively on these films it would be important to pay attention to camera angles, close-ups, jump cuts and other devices by which the audience's experience is structured. For our purpose here, however, we will focus on some of the most prominent aspects of how each film brings the Lear story to a conclusion. They are interestingly different in how they present key events and characters, and how they handle the final moments of the action after Lear's appearance with Cordelia's body. We are going to start with an event we have previously discussed – Edgar and Edmund's trial by combat and its aftermath – to see how Brook's and Nunn's handling of this sequence might make us think about it in a new way.

We noted that, in the text, this is a lengthy sequence and speculated as to why. Is it the moment when justice is re-established, or a moment when the ironic futility of Edgar's efforts to bring justice about is exposed? In Brook's version, Edgar and Edmund both have huge medieval battle axes. Their fight, which occurs in a dark, wind-blown field such that the audience at times can barely see the figures before them, lasts about twenty seconds until Edgar fells his brother with a single blow of this daunting weapon. Edmund dies almost immediately without attempting to prevent the murder of the imprisoned Lear and Cordelia. By contrast, Nunn has the brothers fight with swords, and their highly choreographed duel goes on for several minutes of exciting stage action. After Edgar wins, the film closely follows the text, ending with Edmund's lines about having been loved and meaning to do some good by saving the life of the old King and Cordelia. Take a moment to write about the different effects created by these two versions of the trial by combat, using the following questions as a prompt to your thinking. Does the battle between the two brothers seem like a pivotal event in both films? What is the effect of having it pass by so quickly in the Brook version? Does the brevity of the fight enhance or diminish the sequence's effectiveness? Does the choice of weapon in the two versions matter? Compare how the two films shape how the audience perceives the characters of Edmund and Edgar during the trial by combat and its aftermath. Does either version convey a sense of justice restored? Which version do you prefer and why?

A second major difference between these two films lies in the handling of the women characters in the final scene. In Shakespeare's text, as we noted, all three die offstage. Not so in the Brook film. Almost immediately after Edmund is killed, Goneril kills Regan by throwing her on the ground. In an unforgettable sequence, Goneril then rocks back and forth on her knees, clutching her leather battle outfit. She appears to be in a self-induced trance, and then suddenly throws herself sideways onto a rock, smashing her own skull. As is true of most of the film, close-up shots predominate so that we as audience are looking directly into the faces of every character. After the sisters die, the film cuts to a shot of Cordelia being hung, plunging down until the rope snaps her neck. In Nunn's version, we do not see Cordelia being hung, and both older sisters die offstage, but the camera lingers on a moment when Goneril slips drops of poison into her sister's wine goblet, leading directly to Regan's sudden illness. You will note many other differences in how the women figures are handled in the two versions, starting with the costumes they are given to wear, what happens to their corpses, and the degree to which visual cues suggest their participation in the battle that has just occurred. Gather together your observations about how the two films create distinctive versions of Lear's daughters in this final scene and from those observations make an argument about how their dramatization shapes the audience's experience of each film's conclusion. Which version gives more agency to Goneril and Regan? In which are these women more sexualized? How do such differences affect how the audience experiences the daughters' deaths or assesses their culpability for the chaos in which their world has become enveloped?

Finally, compare how each film handles Lear's appearance onstage carrying the dead body of Cordelia and his subsequent actions. First, write down striking details of each enactment. What are, for example, the most memorable innovations in Brook's treatment of these moments? Think about the flickering images of Cordelia that sporadically appear beside Lear and about the last shot of Lear's head disappearing slowly out of sight in the bottom corner of the screen. How is Brook using these techniques to suggest something about Lear's state of mind, about his relationship to the social world he so long dominated, about his ability to see the truth, whatever that may be? What, by contrast, does Nunn do differently? How does McKellen's speaking of his lines differ from Scofield's? What are the effects each achieves? Where does each actor look when he says: 'Look there, look there' (5.3.310)? What would you argue each director wants to emphasize about the old King as he stands on the verge of death? What questions are answered by the endings each director orchestrates? What questions are perhaps left deliberately unanswered?

Shakespeare's tragedies seldom tidy up the problems they broach. These plays have been described as instruments for thinking and feeling, not machines for producing conclusions. Readers, actors and filmmakers have all turned to *King Lear*, often more than once, because it poses questions that matter, whether those questions have clear answers or not. We have discussed some of them in this book and explored some of the tools you can use to write about them effectively. Now consider what questions *you* most want to address as you conclude your reading journey.

Writing matters

This chapter has taken us to the end of *King Lear*, but it has far from exhausted what we can say about that text. Now is a good moment to reflect on the arc of the whole play and what, in retrospect, you wish to explore further, perhaps in regard to the final act, perhaps in regard to some element of the work that has intrigued you from the very first scene. Here are some prompts to get you started, using some of the tools we have developed throughout this book to begin your brainstorming process. Feel free, of course, to develop your own questions. What have we *not* explored that you feel compelled to engage?

1   What is the most important keyword in *King Lear*? What evidence can you offer to explain and justify your choice?

2   Make an argument about Edgar's role in the final act of this play. How do his actions in 5.2 and in the trial by combat affect how we experience his speaking of the final lines of the play as they are assigned to him in the Folio text? When Edgar speaks these lines, do they provide a satisfying ending to the play? Do they resolve any of the issues the play has explored?

What might they tell us about how Edgar has evolved as a character through the course of the action?

3 By contrast, you might want to argue that the final lines of the play are better given to Albany, as they are in the Quarto version of the play. Go back and revisit the scenes involving Albany in Acts 4 and 5, in particular. Does Albany reveal new aspects of his character in these scenes? How might his speaking of the play's final lines provide a more satisfying sense of an ending than if they are spoken by Edgar?

4 What is signified by Cordelia's speech and silence in the first and last scenes of this play? What themes are developed through her distinctive modes of speech, her reticence and her silence? Can you define Lear's tragic experience in terms of his relationship to these aspects of her behaviour?

5 If you were the director of a stage version of *King Lear*, what are the most important visual impressions you would want to create in the play's final scene? How would you make the most of the visual languages that are a central part of performance?

6 Compare how Peter Brook and Trevor Nunn use the language of dress in the final act of *Lear*. What story do they tell through costume?

7 Who learns anything in *King Lear*? Is this an important question to ask, or should this question be tabled?

CHAPTER FOUR

Writing Skills

Writing is a skill and, as is true of most skills, it can be improved with practice. The more you write, the easier it becomes. The feedback of teachers and peers can also help you get better at defining your argument, finding persuasive evidence to support that argument, and writing clear and compelling prose. As you become increasingly confident as a writer, putting fingers to the keyboard becomes more fun. There are few things more satisfying than deleting three rambling sentences that circle around an idea and replacing them with one sentence that perfectly captures the complexity of the thought you want to express. Writing helps you find out what you really think about a topic; it is also lets you communicate your ideas to a wider audience and persuade others of the value of those ideas. I am always impressed with the sophistication of students' arguments about Shakespeare. Once writers have some basic tools for approaching the verbal complexity and the intricate stagecraft of his plays, their own creativity is released in surprising and wonderful ways. This will be true for you, too.

In what follows I will lay out some general principles for crafting an effective argument about Shakespeare's plays with *King Lear* as the focus. Please know that you do not have to follow all these suggestions in a rote manner. Good essays each have their own unique structures and strategies; however, much of what I am going to suggest has proven effective in aiding the production of a first-rate essay, by which I mean one that is clear, persuasive, and exciting in its implications.

Write about what interests you

There is nothing more likely to produce a dull piece of writing than taking up a topic that does not stir your imagination or challenge you to deal with complexity and contradiction. Always try to land on a topic that raises questions you care about. Are you interested in women's place in early modern society? Or in questions of justice, or of humanity's relationship to the rest of the animal world? Is the morality of disguise a topic that compels you, given the ubiquity of disguise in many Shakespeare plays, including *King Lear*? What about the obligations that come with kingly power, or questions about when authority should be resisted? *King Lear* will lead you into a deep engagement with all of these topics and many others. The point, however, is to find a subject that is of real and pressing interest to you and then to develop it in a way that does justice to its complex unfolding in Shakespeare's tragedy.

Use the observations you have collected through your reading of the play to brainstorm both your topic and the evidence you will use to support it

One of the best ways to find out what really interests you is to engage with a play through short bits of writing focused on the details of its language as we have been doing throughout this book. If you have noted that certain keywords or rhetorical devices are frequently repeated, for example, you might want to unpack those keywords or devices to make a larger point about how they are used and by whom. The same goes for the language of stagecraft. Are there repeated stage gestures, uses of costume or sound effects that open up an interesting line of argument about this play? Does a particular scene seem to you of crucial importance to your interests? What are the features of that scene that you want to discuss? Your relationship to *King Lear* should ideally be dialogic. By this I mean that you come to the text, not as a blank slate, but with interests and preoccupations and critical skills that will in part guide how you read this tragedy and what issues you will foreground. At the same time, the text has material specificity. It is structured in a certain way, uses language in patterned and heightened ways, exists in two textual forms. All of these material factors should shape how you respond to *King Lear* and the kinds of arguments you make about it. As you think about the writing you have already done about the play, try to identify a topic that has seemed especially interesting or crucial to you and list some of the textual nodes where the ideas that compel you are most richly posed or addressed.

Be specific and selective in defining your area of interest but aim for complexity in addressing it

Realize that in a short essay you can't write about everything that compels you in *King Lear*. Instead, narrow your focus, taking up one topic and making a strong argument about it. There is a difference, however, between concentrating on a single subject and making an unnuanced argument about that topic. Shakespeare's plays immerse the reader in complexity and contradiction. None delivers a straightforward 'message' about a problem or an issue. Because plays involve many speaking characters but have no overarching narrative voice as we often find in a novel, the reader frequently must negotiate among the views expressed by different characters on topics ranging from the nature of the gods to the respect that should be paid to elders. Think of the differences between Edmund and Cordelia, for example, on the question of the proper loyalty and respect due to fathers. Each character may make a persuasive case, at least in part, for their beliefs. It is your job to acknowledge the various perspectives the play gives us on a given issue, but then to decide on your own conclusions from among the interpretive possibilities you have unearthed. Your task depends on close engagement, moreover, with Shakespeare's language – his use of metaphors and puns, irony, and complex aural effects that enhance and multiply meaning. We have devoted most of this book to unpacking some of the key textual and performative features of *King Lear*. Consequently, your argument should grow from your engagement with the linguistic sophistication of the text and its implied performance dynamics. You will inevitably find that such an engagement will lead you to the formulation of a nuanced and complex thesis, even if you concentrate on a single topic.

Make your thesis clear and then complicate it as you develop your argument

In the prior paragraph I first discussed identifying a focused topic and then discussed how you develop a complex argument about that topic. This is the journey you will also take as you move through the writing process. After, through brainstorming, you have identified the topic you want to write about and assembled evidence you will consider in addressing that topic, then begin to develop a thesis for your essay. A thesis is an argument you attempt to persuade your reader to accept by marshalling evidence to support your point of view. To engage your reader, a thesis should make a substantial and not a trivial or obvious claim. It is not very compelling, for example, to argue that *King Lear* is notable for its depiction of human suffering. Yes, true, but why is that observation important? Is the suffering of a particular nature? What is the point of this suffering? What conclusions do we draw from the play's depiction of it? Does it reveal the spitefulness of the gods? Is it a result of human viciousness? Are there remedies for it? A good thesis will go beyond the obvious to explain the overarching importance of the claim being advanced. Your thesis should, moreover, be sufficiently complex that it can be developed and complicated in each new section of the essay. Blindness is a verbal trope in *King Lear* and also a physical phenomenon. If you develop a thesis about how blindness functions in this tragedy, each new section of your essay should introduce a new idea and fresh evidence to sustain that overarching thesis. Those new ideas might also lead you to qualify or subtly modify your initial argument. That's fine; in fact, it's a sign that you have really engaged with the text and are letting its complexity spur you to new thoughts. That is what writing does for us as critics: it makes our thinking more rigorous and nuanced.

Develop clear transitions for each new step in your developing argument

One of the hardest things about writing an essay is sequencing your ideas so that a reader is clearly guided from one stage of your thought to the next. If you try to deal with too many ideas in one paragraph, the force of each is diminished or lost. Consequently, you might start with a point that clearly and obviously supports your main argument. Suppose, for example, you wanted to make the argument that in *King Lear* the old King mistreats all his children, that he is, in fact, a kind of domestic tyrant, but that the play nonetheless suggests that children are not therefore justified in dishonouring their fathers. To make such a case, you might start with Lear's mistreatment of his daughter Cordelia during the love test and his violent rhetoric against Goneril and Regan when they also cross his will. This is strong evidence of your first point: that Lear mistreats his daughters.

But then what comes next in your argument? Remember that there will probably be more than one way to proceed. You could address, for example, the strategies by which the play seems to idealize Cordelia in Acts 4 and 5 of the play when she shows herself loyal to Lear even though he has mistreated her and when her acts of kindness in fact jeopardize her life. You could also briefly turn to the subplot and consider Edgar's kindness to Gloucester on their journey to Dover, using the double plot to underscore your main point about how the play elevates children who remain loyal to a parent who has harmed them. Each turn of your argument should be clearly marked with a strong transition sentence telling your reader what is coming next. You might want to conclude, however, with an observation that queries or complicates the argument you have just made. If it is true that the play both reveals Lear's abuse of his children and places a value on filial loyalty, is the cost of such loyalty nonetheless shown to be unacceptably high? When Cordelia returns from France to help her father, she is separated from the husband to whom she once said she owed equal loyalty. Does her death simply return her to the position of self-abnegation that Lear originally, and wrongly, demanded of her? Is this paradox part of what makes this play a tragedy, namely, that it simultaneously shows the incandescence of Lear's rediscovered love for Cordelia and reveals his continuing inability to see the injustice of his demand that Cordelia devote herself only to him and his needs? In making this point, you might want to dig deeply into the language of 5.3.8–19, Lear's speech in which he articulates his wish to live with Cordelia as if they were birds in a cage. It does not matter if Shakespeare 'intended' us to notice this contradiction in his text; we can never know his intentions. What's important is that your work with the text may reveal elements that lead you both to complicate your original thesis and to lay bare what can be seen as that text's own unacknowledged contradictions.

You might well want to make a quite different argument about the Lear–Cordelia relationship, but the point is that, in making any argument, you need to help your reader see clearly each stage of your thinking. Your thesis should include a brief indication of how you will develop your argument, but the body of the essay is where you signpost transitions most fully. It is also where you deal with counter-evidence, that is, parts of the play that seem to contradict your key assertions, and that may therefore lead you to modify or complicate your argument.

Consider multiple forms of evidence to support your argument

The major evidence you will use in composing a Shakespeare essay are the words of his texts. We have spent a lot of time in this book thinking about all the ways you can productively open up the language of *King Lear* to support arguments about the play's many possible meanings. Always quote from the text to support your points and then explain exactly how certain features of the quoted passage create the effects that you say they do. You cannot assume your reader will see what you see in a given passage. Give an account, for example, of *why* repeated imperative verb forms have significance for your argument or *how* end rhyme creates an ironic effect in a particular speech if those are the features you wish to highlight.

Remember, as well, that Shakespeare's plays are more than verbal texts. They also contain cues for embodied performances. They contain stage directions or implied stage directions about non-verbal sounds an audience would hear (such as a storm), gestures an audience would see (such as kneeling), and movements of bodies on- and offstage in sequences that themselves have potential meaning (such as the recurrence of large group scenes in which figures switch places in terms of who is controlling the actions of the others). As we saw in Chapter 3, nothing mandates that an actual performance of the play will follow either the text or the implied performance cues embedded in the text. Performances are interpretations that realize the text in various ways. Nonetheless, thinking of the text in relationship to performance possibilities is one way of keeping alive the recognition that theatre is a three-dimensional art form and the evidence you adduce to support your thesis may involve kinetic, visual and aural, as well as verbal, phenomena.

There are also some important scholarly tools you can consult to help you gather evidence for your thesis. The online version of the *Oxford English Dictionary* is, as we discussed earlier, an important tool for figuring out the several meanings a word could have in the early modern period and also for showing how a word's meanings change over time. This information can provide crucial evidence for claims you might want to make about how a word functions in a particular passage. Similarly, for some purposes you might want to consult a reference work such as Gordon Williams's *A Dictionary of Sexual Language and Imagery in Shakespearean and Stuart Literature*. Shakespeare frequently employed sexual puns and wordplay, and many speeches in *King Lear* have bawdy undercurrents. Williams teases out the sexual meanings of this language, which may help you develop a line of argument about, for example, the ways Lear's negative attitudes towards women are expressed in a language of sexual disgust. Also helpful is Alan Dessen and Leslie Thomson's *A Dictionary of Stage Directions in English Drama, 1580–1642*. This handy book explains the specialized vocabulary sometimes used in early modern printed stage directions and gives many examples of particular objects, actions and sounds found in these stage directions.

What about the many books of criticism, as opposed to reference works, that address Shakespeare's plays? Do they provide evidence for arguments you might want to make? This is a good question and one with no simple answer. When we read criticism, it can help us see how others make arguments about Shakespeare's plays; it can also widen the range of topics we might consider engaging through his works. However, it is unproductive to let other critics do your thinking for you. When you cite another critic, do so briefly, and make clear what idea in their work has been a useful spur to your own thinking. Then move quickly to highlight how you are extending, contradicting or complicating that critic's line of argument. In your first engagements with Shakespeare it is always best to strike out on your own rather than relying primarily on the ideas of others. In this book you have developed a toolkit of questions and critical strategies that allow you to read with confidence and sophistication. Use those tools to develop your arguments, rather than relying primarily on the interpretive skill of others.

Pay attention to developing a strong conclusion

Some writers find conclusions the hardest part of an argument because they see them primarily as a repetition, in shorter form, of an argument they have already made. Such repetition would indeed make for a dull conclusion. Instead, while you may want to remind your reader of the main points you have made in support of your thesis, an effective conclusion will do much more. It will, for example, make clear the *stakes* of the argument: why what you have argued is important, how it challenges mainstream interpretations of the play, what light it sheds on the differences between the early modern time period and our own. An effective conclusion can also put a new spin on some part of the argument you have already made as I suggested in the section on transitions above. While you don't want to undermine the main thrust of the argument you have been building, you may want to take a final step in which you point out an unforeseen consequence of that argument or a further question it raises. There is seldom a last word in writing about Shakespeare, and a good conclusion may find a way to demonstrate that fact.

Revise

It should come as no surprise that nearly all writers spend as much time revising as working on their initial draft of an essay. That is usually because ideas change as you write about them and work with the evidence you have gathered to support your thesis. Sometimes, for example, an initial thesis will come to seem too simple to account for all the evidence and counter-evidence you have discovered. Alternatively, it may become evident that you do not need every element you included in your first draft. In fact, the essay might be more effective if some parts were cut or the essay's structure changed. Whatever your revision involves, it's important to be open to the possibility of significantly altering your first draft. As you read it over, ask yourself first if its basic argument still seems persuasive to you. If not, what changes would make it more convincing? Second, is the essay organized effectively? Should some of the material be cut or shifted around and new transitions created? Third, ask yourself if you have marshalled the best evidence to support your thesis. If not, what could you add? Fourth, is there any counter-evidence which you have not taken into account. If so, how will you address it? Finally, have you written a conclusion that is more than a repetition of prior points? How have you used those final pages to broaden the implications of the argument or to delineate its stakes? Be sure to give yourself time to go through these steps so that your final draft expresses your best thinking on your topic.

Pay attention to accuracy and to the conventions governing academic writing

Throughout the process of writing, but especially when working on your final draft, be sure all quotations are accurately transcribed and that you provide act, scene and line numbers for any passage you quote from *King Lear*. Don't make your reader hunt for the lines you are quoting. Be equally careful with your own prose. Check the spelling of hard or unfamiliar words; be sure you have no run-on sentences or sentence fragments; review the accuracy of your punctuation and of formatting conventions. A concern for accuracy and tight, grammatical prose helps your readers focus on your ideas rather than on silently amending errors; it also prevents them from getting lost in confusing and rambling sentences. You and only you are responsible for the argument you are making and also for the effective communication of that argument. Attending to the conventions of good writing is part of the task.

Proofread

Finally, when you are satisfied with your thesis and the way you have structured your essay and marshalled your evidence, when you have checked your quotations and addressed any errors of punctuation, grammar and sentence structure, read the whole thing over one last time to be sure you have caught any lingering errors or hard-to-follow sentences. And then just enjoy your accomplishment.

BIBLIOGRAPHY

Anderson, David K. 'The Tragedy of Good Friday: Sacrificial Violence in
    King Lear', *English Literary History* 78.2 (2011), 259–86. Argues that
    King Lear depicts the bodily suffering of Gloucester and Cordelia in
    light of Reformation debates about religious violence, and that the
    play thus manifests early modern England's ambivalent attitude
    towards sacrificial violence.
Adelman, Janet. *Suffocating Mothers: Fantasies of Maternal Origin in
    Shakespeare's Plays, 'Hamlet' to 'The Tempest'* (New York: Routledge,
    1992), 103–29. Explores how Shakespeare's plays depict masculinity
    as threatened by femininity, by the maternal body in particular.
    Chapter 5 reads Lear's madness in light of early modern theories of
    female hysteria, suggesting that his desire for union with Cordelia
    stems from an early, ungendered form of selfhood that longs for
    maternal consolation.
Aguiar, Sarah Appleton. '(Dis)Obedient Daughters: (Dis)Inheriting the
    Kingdom of Lear', in Mica Howe and Sarah Appleton Aguiar (eds),
    He Said, She Says: An RSVP to the Male Text (Madison, NJ: Fairleigh
    Dickinson University Press, 2001), 194–210. A survey of feminist
    rewritings of *King Lear* in contemporary novels by Margaret Atwood,
    Laura Esquivel, Jane Smiley and Anne Tyler.
Berger, Harry. *Making Trifles of Terrors: Redistributing Complicities in
    Shakespeare* (Stanford: Stanford University Press, 1997), 25–69.
    Chapters 3 and 4 examine family relationships in *Lear*, drawing upon
    a range of methods from character analysis to psychological criticism,
    to consider the influence of language upon ethics.
Berry, Philippa. *Shakespeare's Feminine Endings: Disfiguring Death in the
    Tragedies* (New York: Routledge, 1999), 135–66. Argues that
    Shakespeare's tragedies, employing a range of images and tropes
    related to mutability and absence, feminize death. Chapter 6 treats the
    question of territorial integrity in *Lear* in light of King James's project
    of unifying England and Scotland and traces the ways in which
    Cordelia's body emblematizes both a fissured and a reconciled state.
Booth, Stephen. *'King Lear', 'Macbeth', Indefinition and Tragedy* (New
    Haven: Yale University Press, 1983). Treats tragedy, and *King Lear*

especially, as uniquely prone to produce effects of indeterminacy and inconclusiveness, arguing that precise and patterned language paradoxically plays an important role in this process.

Brooks, Douglas A. 'King Lear (1608) and the Typography of Literary Ambition', Renaissance Drama 30 (1999–2001), 133–59. Studies the Quarto from the perspective of textual studies and book history, moving beyond playwrights and theatrical companies to consider the 1608 Lear in light of the important work performed by printers.

Buchanan, Judith. Shakespeare on Film (London: Longman, 2005). Surveys the history of Shakespeare in cinema, from silent film to the present, touching on King Lear throughout and devoting particular attention to two notable adaptations: Akira Kurosawa's 1985 film Ran, and Kristian Levring's 2000 The King is Alive.

Cavell, Stanley. Disowning Knowledge in Seven Plays of Shakespeare, 2nd edn (Cambridge: Cambridge University Press, 2003), 39–124. Chapter 2 argues that the tragedy of King Lear springs from the desire to avoid being recognized by others, with searching readings of Lear's avoidance of being recognized by his daughters and the disguised Edgar's avoidance of being recognized by Gloucester.

Callaghan, Dympna. Woman and Gender in Renaissance Tragedy: A Study of 'King Lear', 'Othello', 'The Duchess of Malfi' and 'The White Devil' (Atlantic Highlands, NJ: Humanities Press International, 1989). Explores the relationship between tragedy and gender by tracing thematic continuities between several Shakespearean tragedies, including King Lear, paying special attention to female silence, absence and transgression.

Carroll, William C. Fat King, Lean Beggar: Representations of Poverty in the Age of Shakespeare (Ithaca: Cornell University Press, 1996), 180–207. Examines Poor Tom as a complex figure who thematically links two of the play's important pairings: Edgar and Edmund, and Gloucester and Lear. Argues that the body of the beggar partly destabilizes social hierarchies since it both elicits sympathy from Lear and bears a resemblance to Lear's own body.

Cartelli, Thomas. Repositioning Shakespeare: National Formations, Postcolonial Appropriations (New York: Routledge, 1999), 46–62. Examines how national and postcolonial contexts open new interpretive possibilities for reading Shakespeare. Chapter 2 looks at how the pioneering social worker Jane Addams appropriated the Lear story to illuminate an 1894 labour strike.

Croall, Jonathan. Performing King Lear: Gielgud to Russell Beale (London: The Arden Shakespeare, 2015). An account of the difficulties and possibilities of staging King Lear based on interviews with twenty actors who played Lear and two dozen directors who staged the play in the last fifty to sixty years.

De Grazia, Margreta. 'The Ideology of Superfluous Things: *King Lear* as a Period Piece', in Margreta de Grazia, Maureen Quilligan and Peter Stallybrass (eds), *Subject and Object in Renaissance Culture* (Cambridge: Cambridge University Press, 1996), 17–42. Analyses the play with special attention to class and periodization, exploring the ways in which *King Lear* presents personhood and property as inseparable.

Dessen, Alan C., and Leslie Thomson. *A Dictionary of Stage Directions in English Drama, 1580–1642* (Cambridge: Cambridge University Press, 1999). A comprehensive examination of the stage directions found in the plays of Shakespeare and his contemporaries.

Dodd, William. 'Impossible Worlds: What Happens in *King Lear*, Act 1, Scene 1?' *Shakespeare Quarterly* 50.4 (1999), 477–507. Discusses the love test that Lear asks his daughters to perform and Cordelia's relationship to Kent, paying particular attention to the way that verbal interaction creates interlocutors.

Dollimore, Jonathan. *Radical Tragedy: Religion, Ideology, and Power in the Drama of Shakespeare and His Contemporaries*, 3rd edn (New York: Palgrave Macmillan, 2004), 189–203. Offers a materialist reading in which *King Lear* is not a play about the redemptive suffering inherent to human nature, but about the interaction of power, property and inheritance.

Drakakis, John, ed. *Shakespearean Tragedy* (London: Longman, 1992). Contains essays by Terry Eagleton, Malcolm Evans, Marilyn French and Alessandro Sarpieri who read *King Lear* in light of subjects that range from gender and genre to politics and semiotics.

Erickson, Peter. *Patriarchal Structures in Shakespeare's Drama* (Berkeley: University of California Press, 1985). Explores the relationship between male bonding and patriarchy, treating *Lear* alongside male pairings in *Hamlet* and *Othello*.

Foakes, R. A. *Hamlet Versus Lear: Cultural Politics and Shakespeare's Art* (Cambridge: Cambridge University Press, 1993). Surveys the intertwined critical reception of *Hamlet* and *King Lear* over two centuries, arguing that critical praise has tipped towards *Lear* in the last half-century on account of political upheavals that left *Lear* uniquely positioned to speak to today's world.

Freeman, Donald C. '"According to My Bond": *King Lear* and Re-cognition', *Language and Literature* 2.1 (1993), 1–18. Considers how cognitive metaphors of balancing and linking connect to embodied, real-world experience, and so explores the way that figurative language shapes both Lear's understanding of the world and the reader's understanding of the play.

Gottlieb, Christine M. '"Unaccommodated Man": Dismodernism and Disability Justice in *King Lear*', *Disability Studies Quarterly* 38.4 (Fall

2018). Uses a disability studies lens to show how Lear comes to understand the fundamental interdependency of human life.

Greenblatt, Stephen. *Shakespearean Negotiations: The Circulation of Social Energy in Renaissance England* (Berkeley: University of California Press, 1988), 94–128. Chapter 4 reads the Poor Tom scenes in light of a source text, Samuel Harsnett's *A Declaration of Egregious Popish Impostures*, to show how theatre empties out the belief structures it stages.

Griggs, Yvonne. *Screen Adaptations: Shakespeare's King Lear, The Relationship Between Text and Film* (London: Methuen Drama, 2009). Surveys a wide range of *Lear* films and offers critical readings of both traditional and experimental adaptations.

Gross, Kenneth. *Shakespeare's Noise* (Chicago: The University of Chicago Press, 2001), 161–92. Chapter 6 examines the function of curses in *King Lear*, arguing that Lear's curses fall back on himself.

Hadfield, Andrew. 'The Power and Rights of the Crown in *Hamlet* and *King Lear*: "The King – The King's to Blame"', *Review of English Studies* 54.217 (2003), 566–86. Explores these two tragedies as commentaries on the question of monarchic succession, offering the court of James I as a model of undesirable succession.

Hamilton, Jennifer Mae. *This Contentious Storm: An Ecocritical and Performance History of* King Lear (London: Bloomsbury, 2017). Combines critical analysis of *King's Lear*'s storm and its ecological effects with a detailed survey of how the storm has been staged across four centuries.

Hamlin, Hannibal. *The Bible in Shakespeare* (Oxford: Oxford University Press, 2013), 305–33. Explores the constellation of allusions to the Book of Job in *King Lear*, looking at how the language and beliefs associated with the Job story were shared with a number of other influential early modern authors, including John Calvin and Christopher Marlowe.

Hoeniger, F. David. *Medicine and Shakespeare in the English Renaissance* (Newark, DE: University of Delaware Press, 1992). Studies the impact of early modern medical thought on Shakespeare's plays, offering an essay that reads Lear's madness in this context.

Höfele, Andreas. *Stage, Stake, and Scaffold: Humans and Animals in Shakespeare's Theatre* (Oxford: Oxford University Press, 2011), 171–228. Argues that the sovereign in *King Lear* is himself a threat to civility and that man's superiority over the beasts is repeatedly called into question by the play's action.

Holahan, Michael. '"Look, Her Lips": Softness of Voice, Construction of Character in *King Lear*', *Shakespeare Quarterly* 48.4 (1997), 406–31. Looks at the construction of character as an effect of rhetoric in Lear's speech over Cordelia's body, an act that reappraises her earlier silence during the love contest by imitating her soft voice.

Holland, Peter, ed. *'King Lear' and Its Afterlife. Shakespeare Survey*
55 (2002). A collection of essays broadly surveying recent critical
assessments of *King Lear*. The many engaging essays include: Kiernan
Ryan charting critical approaches to *Lear* from the 1980s onwards;
William C. Carroll documenting the popularity of 'Mad Tom' ballads
in *Lear* and beyond; Andrew Gurr treating the play's use of headgear
from the perspective of theatre history; and Peter Womack examining
Lear's Restoration adaptation by Nahum Tate.

Hoxby, Blair. *What was Tragedy?: Theory and the Early Modern Canon*
(Oxford: Oxford University Press, 2015), 79–84. Argues that tragedy
was understood in early modern Europe not as a form dominated by
character and action, but by the imitation of passions and emotions.
Chapter 2 tests this theory against a number of early modern tragedies,
including *King Lear*.

Jorgens, Jack. *Shakespeare on Film* (Bloomington: Indiana University
Press, 1977), 235–51. Chapter 16 compares Peter Brook's existential
tale of meaningless violence with Grigori Kozintsev's more positive
story of Christian redemption.

Kahan, Jeffrey, ed. *King Lear: New Critical Essays* (New York: Routledge,
2008). Eleven short essays aimed at tracing the range of recent
responses to central interpretive problems in the play.

Kahn, Paul W. *Law and Love: The Trials of King Lear* (New Haven: Yale
University Press, 2000). Examines the supposedly transhistorical
lessons that *Lear* has to offer about the dialectic between law and love,
especially as this plays out in the language of different characters.

Kermode, Frank. *Shakespeare's Language* (New York: Farrar, Strauss and
Giroux, 2000), 183–200. A study of Shakespeare's style and rhetorical
formulae; the essay devoted to *King Lear* charts linguistic patterns and
images that are particular to individual characters, themes, and phases
of dramatic action.

Kerrigan, John. *Shakespeare's Binding Language* (Oxford: Oxford
University Press, 2016), 336–66. Chapter 13 treats the language of gifts,
lending, debt, benefits and oaths in *King Lear* and *Timon of Athens*.

Khan, Coppélia. 'The Absent Mother in *King Lear*', in Margaret W.
Ferguson, Maureen Quilligan and Nancy Vickers (eds), *Rewriting the
Renaissance: The Discourses of Sexual Differences in Early Modern
Europe* (Chicago: The University of Chicago Press, 1986), 33–49. A
feminist and psychoanalytic reading of gender and the family,
including the influence of a 'maternal subtext' upon the male psyche.

Kronenfeld, Judy. *'King Lear' and the Naked Truth: Rethinking the
Language of Religion and Resistance* (Durham, NC: Duke University
Press, 1998). Argues that the key to interpretation of *King Lear* is not
recent critical trends but Christian culture, and the cultural vocabulary
that originally gave it meaning.

Leggatt, Alexander. *King Lear, Shakespeare in Performance*, 2nd edn
    (Manchester: Manchester University Press, 2004). Surveys a range of
    present-day performance practices, from stage productions to films, as
    they impact the critical and interpretive possibilities in *Lear*.
Lehmann, Courtney. '"A Wail in the Silence": Feminism, Sexuality and
    Final Meanings in *King Lear* Films by Grigori Kozintsev, Peter Brook,
    and Akira Kurosawa', in Russell Jackson (ed.), *The Cambridge
    Companion to Shakespeare on Screen* (Cambridge: Cambridge
    University Press, 2020), 161–72. Treats the gender dynamics of three
    film versions of *Lear*, arguing that the play shows how little room
    women have in a patriarchal culture.
Lupton, Julia Reinhard, and Kenneth Reinhard. *After Oedipus:
    Shakespeare in Psychoanalysis* (Ithaca: Cornell University Press, 1993),
    145–247. Reads nothingness in *Lear* in light of both Lacan and Freud
    as well as the Book of Job, charting intersections between the feminine
    and the unrepresentable.
Mack, Maynard. *King Lear in Our Time* (Berkeley: University of
    California Press, 1965). Reads the play for its mixture of archetypal
    elements from the morality drama, parable and dream vision and
    realistic, homely language.
Magnusson, Lynne. *Shakespeare and Social Dialogue: Dramatic Language
    and Elizabethan Letters* (Cambridge: Cambridge University Press,
    1999), 141–53. Examines way in which the conversational exchanges
    that shape social identities are disrupted in *King Lear* as conversations
    fail the fundamental test of acknowledging others.
Marx, Steven. *Shakespeare and the Bible* (Oxford: Oxford University
    Press, 2000), 59–78. Treats a long-standing topic: the influence of the
    Book of Job on *Lear*, looking at both linguistic parallels as well as the
    role of revision in later versions of both texts.
Martin, Christopher. *Constituting Old Age in Early Modern English
    Literature, from Queen Elizabeth to 'King Lear'* (Amherst, MA:
    University of Massachusetts Press, 2012). Treats *King Lear* as a
    turning point in early modern representations of old age and
    revisits the key theme of sight in light of the complicated term
    'spectacle', which denotes both an instrument the elderly use to
    see as well as the ridiculous show into which the rising generation
    would make them.
McEachern, Claire. *Believing in Shakespeare: Studies in Longing*
    (Cambridge: Cambridge University Press, 2018), 225–75. Considers how
    the problem of religious belief in Shakespeare's world informed the
    problem of believing in the fictional world onstage. Chapter 6 focuses on
    the many inconsistencies of plot in *King Lear* and how Shakespeare
    induces the audience to experience dread at the play's impending
    catastrophe.

McLuskie, Kate. 'The Patriarchal Bard: Feminist Criticism and Shakespeare: *King Lear* and *Measure for Measure*', in Jonathan Dollimore and Alan Sinfield (eds), *Political Shakespeare: Essays in Cultural Materialism*, 2nd edn (Ithaca: Cornell University Press, 1994), 88–108. Suggests how the play resists feminist readings, since it so often makes it impossible for the audience to identify with female characters like Goneril and Regan, leaving patriarchal structures as an implicit defence against chaos.

Mentz, Steve. 'Strange Weather in *King Lear*', *Shakespeare* 6.2 (2010), 139–52. Argues that depictions of the weather in *King Lear* point towards a radical disequilibrium in which human bodies and the natural world alike are characterized by ceaseless change.

Minor, Benjamin, and Ayanna Thompson. '"Edgar I Nothing Am": Blackface in *King Lear*', in Rory Loughnane and Edel Semple (eds), *Staged Transgression in Shakespeare's England* (New York: Palgrave Macmillan, 2013), 153–64. Discusses the possible ways in which Edgar, especially in his role as Poor Tom, is racially coded.

Miola, Robert S. *Shakespeare's Reading* (Oxford: Oxford University Press, 2000), 109–16. Examines *The True Chronicle History of King Leir* as a source for *King Lear*, noting how Shakespeare alters the source by such things as the inclusion of a subplot and the character of the Fool, as well as by changing the ending so that Cordelia dies and Lear loses the battle against France.

Mooney, Michael E. *Shakespeare's Dramatic Transactions* (Durham, NC: Duke University Press, 1990), 129–49. Examines the multiple functions of the character Edgar, including the way in which his language and stage position allow him to address and engage the audience.

Neill, Michael, and David Schalkwyk, eds. *The Oxford Handbook of Shakespearean Tragedy* (Oxford: Oxford University Press, 2016). Collection of more than fifty essays on Shakespeare's tragedies. Contributions with a special focus on *King Lear* include Gail Kern Paster on Lear's embodiment; Leah S. Marcus on the place of nature in the play; Bridget Escolme on twentieth- and twenty-first-century stage productions; and MacDonald P. Jackson on film versions.

Nowottny, Winifred. 'Some Aspects of the Style of *King Lear*', *Shakespeare Survey* 13 (1960), 49–57. Examines the juxtaposition of ornate and simple speech in the play and the disproportion between the huge emotional stakes of the action and the homely language in which they are often expressed.

Orkin, Martin. 'Cruelty, *King Lear*, and the South African Land Act 1913', *Shakespeare Survey* 40 (1988), 135–44. Discusses class and the division of land in *King Lear* and considers how those issues resonate for readers in apartheid South Africa.

Palfrey, Simon. *Poor Tom: Living* King Lear (Chicago: The University of Chicago Press, 2014). A multifaceted exploration of Edgar, his disguise as Poor Tom, and that figure's centrality to our understanding of the play.

Palfrey, Simon, and Tiffany Stern. *Shakespeare in Parts* (Oxford: Oxford University Press, 2007), 240–65. Explores dramatic texts from the perspective of the 'part', the portion of the script used by individual actors in early modern theatre companies and looks at cue lines in *Lear* – lines spoken by one actor as a prompt for another actor to enter or speak.

Patterson, Annabel. *Shakespeare and the Popular Voice* (Cambridge, MA: Basil Blackwell, 1989), 93–119. Explores Shakespeare's interest in common, working people; points to moments of populist critique in his plays; and in Chapter 5 includes a discussion of Lear himself as a social critic.

Phelan, Peggy. 'Reconstructing Love: *King Lear* and Theatre Architecture', in Barbara Hodgdon and W. B. Worthen (eds), *A Companion to Shakespeare and Performance* (Malden, MA: Blackwell Publishing, 2005), 13–35. Reflects on *King Lear*'s spaces, including the map and the hovel, in light of how theatrical space explores the boundary between the real and the theatrical.

Procházka, Martin, Michael Neill, and David Schalkwyk, eds. *Versions of* King Lear, special issue of *Litteraria Pragensia* 26.52 (December 2016). Collection of essays on adaptations and reuses of *King Lear*, from Nahum Tate's Restoration revision to the present day.

Pye, Christopher. *The Vanishing: Shakespeare, the Subject, and Early Modern Culture* (Durham, NC: Duke University Press, 2000), 65–104. Re-evaluates materialist understandings of the self from a psychoanalytic perspective, focusing in Chapter 3 on the role of performance in the Dover Cliff scene.

Reynolds, Paige Martin. *Performing Shakespeare's Women: Playing Dead* (London: The Arden Shakespeare, 2019), 41–64. Chapter 2 draws on Reynolds's own experience as an actor playing Regan to consider how the play treats its female characters and the actors who portray them.

Rosenberg, Marvin. *The Masks of King Lear* (Berkeley: University of California Press, 1972). Examines the performance possibilities of every scene in the play in light of prior performances and critical history.

Rothwell, Kenneth S. *A History of Shakespeare on Screen: A Century of Film and Television*, 2nd edn (Cambridge: Cambridge University Press, 2004). Touches on most major screen performances of *Lear*.

Rutter, Carol Chillington. *Enter the Body: Women and Representation on Shakespeare's Stage* (New York: Routledge, 2001), 1–26. Examines the way performing bodies can interrupt and exceed the meanings conveyed by Shakespeare's language. Chapter 1 studies the gendering of death in *Lear* through the living bodies that perform Cordelia's corpse.

Schalkwyk, David. *Speech and Performance in Shakespeare's Sonnets and Plays* (Cambridge: Cambridge University Press, 2002), 102–49. Examines *King Lear* alongside *Hamlet* and several sonnets to argue that *Lear* offers an unusual view of the capacity for spoken words to access interiority, centring his reading on the 'language games' between Lear and Cordelia.

Schalkwyk, David. *Shakespeare, Love and Service* (Cambridge: Cambridge University Press, 2008), 214–62. Studies the affective conditions and social structures that make love and service overlapping concepts in Shakespeare's drama, with special attention to the master–servant relationship between Kent and Lear.

Shaheen, Naseeb. *Biblical References in Shakespeare's Plays* (Newark, DE: University of Delaware Press, 1999), 604–20. Catalogues the plethora of biblical and liturgical allusions in Shakespeare's plays; pages 604–20 focus on *Lear*.

Shannon, Laurie. *The Accommodated Animal: Cosmopolity in Shakespearean Locales* (Chicago: The University of Chicago Press, 2013), 127–73. Offers a posthumanist reading of *King Lear* in which Shannon sees *Lear* participating in a 'zoographic' counter-tradition to human exceptionalism, in which view the play's concern with themes of human hardship and sovereignty draws on a sense of animal vulnerability.

Shapiro, James. *The Year of Lear: Shakespeare in 1606* (New York: Simon & Schuster, 2015). Reads the play, as well as *Macbeth* and *Antony and Cleopatra*, against the background of political paranoia in England following Guy Fawkes's attempted 'gunpowder plot' in November 1605.

Spevack, Marvin. *The Harvard Concordance to Shakespeare* (Cambridge, MA: The Belknap Press of Harvard University Press, 1973). Provides a listing of all the words in Shakespeare and the places and frequency of their occurrence.

Strier, Richard. *Resistant Structures: Particularity, Radicalism, and Renaissance Texts* (Berkeley: University of California Press, 1995), 165–202. Examines the dilemma faced by those bound to obey a wicked authority, contending that Shakespeare advances a radical view in which 'good service' resists authority in favour of virtuous action. Essay 8 extends its political reading to Nahum Tate's Restoration adaptation of *King Lear*.

Taylor, Gary, and Michael Warren, eds. *The Division of the Kingdoms: Shakespeare's Two Versions of* King Lear (Oxford: Clarendon Press, 1983). Essays influential in developing the view that the Folio revisions are authorial in origin. Shows how the concerns of textual studies, from changes in spelling and speaker to the presence or absence of a given passage, impact critical readings of the play.

Traub, Valerie. 'The Nature of Norms in Early Modern England: Anatomy, Cartography, *King Lear*', *South Central Review* 26.1–2 (2009), 42–81. Shows how *King Lear* engages with and contributes to early modern scientific discourses that sought to classify and differentiate human bodies according to a 'logic of the grid' that worked to establish categories of normality.

Turner, Henry S. *The English Renaissance Stage: Geometry, Poetics, and the Practical Spatial Arts, 1580–1630* (Oxford: Oxford University Press, 2006), 155–85. Considers a range of spatial effects in *Lear*, from those suggested by the role of cartography within the play, to those produced by the play's existence on both the printed page and theatrical stage.

Urkowitz, Steven. *Shakespeare's Revision of King Lear* (Princeton: Princeton University Press, 1980). Lays out the changes between the 1608 Quarto and 1623 Folio, carefully noting textual variants, in order to advance the view that the Folio is a purposeful revision of the Quarto.

Vickers, Brian. *The One* King Lear (Cambridge, MA: Harvard University Press, 2016). Controversial argument against the view that the Quarto and Folio texts reflect Shakespeare's revisions, positing instead that Shakespeare wrote one version of the play that was improperly printed in both texts.

Williams, Gordon. *A Glossary of Shakespeare's Sexual Language* (London: Athlone Press, 1997). Lists and explains an astonishing number of Shakespearean words with sexual meanings.

Wittreich, Joseph. '*Image of that Horror*': History, Prophecy, and Apocalypse in King Lear (San Marino, CA: The Huntington Library, 1984). Studies the apocalyptic framework informing *Lear*, arguing that the play despite its grimness offers hope for a renewed world.

Editions

Foakes, R. A., ed. *King Lear*. The Arden Shakespeare Third Series. London: The Arden Shakespeare, 1997.

Greenblatt, Stephen, Walter Cohen, Suzanne Gossett, Jean E. Howard, Katharine Eisaman Maus, and Gordon McMullan, eds. *The Norton Shakespeare*. Third Edition. New York: W.W. Norton & Co., 2016.

Halio, Jay L., ed. *The First Quarto of King Lear*. New Cambridge Shakespeare: Early Quartos. Cambridge: Cambridge University Press, 1994.

Hinman, Charlton, ed. *The First Folio of Shakespeare*. Norton Facsimile. Second Edition. New York: W.W. Norton & Co., 1996.

Ioppolo, Grace. *King Lear*. Norton Critical Editions. New York: W.W. Norton & Co., 2008.

Mowat, Barbara A., and Paul Werstine, eds. *The Tragedy of King Lear*. Folger Digital Texts: http://www.folgerdigitaltexts.org/html/Lr.html

Weis, René, ed. *King Lear: A Parallel Text Edition*. Second Edition. New York: Routledge, 2013.

Wells, Stanley, ed. *The History of King Lear*. The Oxford Shakespeare. Oxford: Oxford University Press, 2000.

Film and television adaptations

King Lear. Directed by William V. Ranous. 1909. Vitagraph.
Korol Lir. Directed by Grigori Kozintsev. 1970. Lenfilm Studio.
King Lear. Directed by Peter Brook. 1971. Athéna Films.
King Lear. Directed by Jean-Luc Godard. 1987. Cannon Films.
King Lear. Directed by Trevor Nunn. 2008. Pinewood Studios. PBS Video.
Ran. Directed by Akira Kurosawa. 1985. Greenwich Film Production, Herald Ace, Inc., Nippon Herald Films.
The King is Alive. Directed by Kristian Levring. 2000. Newmarket Capital Group.

Websites

The Bodleian First Folio: http://firstfolio.bodleian.ox.ac.uk
The British Library: Shakespeare in Quarto. http://www.bl.uk/treasures/shakespeare/homepage.html Includes quarto texts and basic background information about the play, Shakespeare and early modern theatre.
Global Shakespeares: http://globalshakespeares.mit.edu Features recordings of stage productions and adaptations from around the world, including eighteen of *Lear* at this time.
Holinshed Project: http://www.cems.ox.ac.uk/holinshed/ Includes a digital copy of the 1587 edition of the *Chronicles*, and background information about Holinshed and history writing.
King Lear: Folger Shakespeare Library: http://www.folger.edu/king-lear Includes links to facsimiles of quartos and folios of *King Lear*, and to an image database of scenic and costume designs, promotional and commemorative illustrations, manuscript materials and more, mostly from the eighteenth and nineteenth centuries.
The Map of Early Modern London: https://mapoflondon.uvic.ca
Shakespearean London Theatres: http://shalt.dmu.ac.uk/index.html